THE BRONTËS
AND OTHER
ESSAYS

THE BRONTËS
AND OTHER
ESSAYS

By

GODFREY FOX BRADBY

Essay Index Reprint Series

Originally published by:

OXFORD UNIVERSITY PRESS

BOOKS FOR LIBRARIES PRESS, INC.
FREEPORT, NEW YORK

First Published 1932
Reprinted 1967

Reprinted from a copy in the collections of
The New York Public Library
Astor, Lenox and Tilden Foundations

LIBRARY OF CONGRESS CATALOG NUMBER:
67-30176

PRINTED IN THE UNITED STATES OF AMERICA

Acknowledgement

THE Essay on Emily Brontë appeared first in *The Nineteenth Century* and is included here by the kind permission of the Editor of that magazine

Contents

1. *Charlotte Brontë and Mr. Nicholls*

THE Brontë letters fill two large volumes.[1] With comparatively few exceptions they are Charlotte's letters, and of these by far the greater number were written to the most intimate of her rare friends, Miss Ellen Nussey, who had first come into her life at the school at Roe Head, and who remained in close touch with her till death parted them. These letters tell us most of what we know about Charlotte Brontë and her family; but they do not tell us everything. With a pen in her hand Charlotte could be gloriously indiscreet; but her indiscretion stopped at the gate of Haworth Parsonage. When her father or her brother and sisters were a part of the story, she generally practised an admirable but rather tantalizing reserve, and, where she had a secret of her own to keep, she could be as silent as the grave. Had it been otherwise there would be far fewer Brontë problems to exercise the imagination of Brontë enthusiasts. The story of Branwell's downfall might present no difficulties, Emily would be less of an enigma, and we should know how long Charlotte's infatuation for M. Heger survived the ordeal of absence, and how much or how little she loved Mr. Nicholls when she knelt beside him on her wedding day in Haworth Church. As it is, much of the Brontë history is wrapped in mystery.

[1] *The Brontës. Life and Letters.* By Clement Shorter. 1908.

And if Charlotte is not always revealing, she is sometimes positively misleading. For, although she was a splendidly truthful woman, both in speech and in her determination to recognize facts and to face them, she did not always see straight. From her earliest years she was a shrewd judge of character, but not often a friendly one. She had certain obvious limitations (some of them, no doubt, due in part to her physical disabilities) which sometimes impaired her judgement. She was inclined to be censorious; she mistook grey for black; and, like many people who are lavish in their dispraise of others, she was morbidly sensitive to any criticism of herself. As a governess she was a failure. She was never really fond of children, and when they were naughty, she thought that they were depraved. In her employers she could find nothing good. If they tried to be kind, they were condescending; if they left her alone, they despised her; if they ventured to offer advice, she took it as an affront. Women who are determined to feel slighted, and whose health is permanently below par, do not, however talented they may be, make good governesses.

Misleading, too, is Charlotte's epistolary attitude towards her father and her aunt. She believed in parental authority. In practice, as well as on paper, she was a dutiful daughter and a dutiful niece. She never criticized her father or her aunt in her letters as she criticized her friends and acquaintances. In theory their joint will was law in the Brontë household; and there were occasions on which it was not inconvenient to invoke their authority. If, for example, it was Ellen Nussey's turn to visit the Parsonage and she wanted Charlotte to come to Brookroyd instead, Charlotte, who was sensitive on matters of etiquette, and always ready to suspect some slight to Haworth, would reply that, whatever her personal inclinations might be, Papa and Aunt were strongly opposed to the proposal, and that it must therefore be abandoned. As a matter of fact, whatever she might say or think, when Charlotte wanted anything badly, she generally succeeded in getting her own way; she triumphed, not by open revolt, but by a masterful persuasiveness. When she chose, Charlotte could manage her elders as quietly and as firmly as she managed her sisters.

In this connexion it may be permissible to say a word about Miss Branwell, because her memory has suffered some wrong at the hands of those who are convinced that, because the Brontë girls possessed genius, they necessarily had a thwarted and unhappy childhood. It is customary to present her as a rather grim and unsympathetic martinet, to poke fun at her pattens, her old-fashioned gowns and her old-fashioned ways, and to suggest that she kept her nieces eternally occupied with tasks which were wholly unsuited to their precocious talents.

The simple facts are these. Miss Branwell came to Haworth in 1821, to keep house for her brother-in-law and to look after his motherless children.

In doing so she knowingly exchanged her sunny home in Cornwall, her circle of old friends and acquaintances, her tea parties, and her independence, for a climate that she did not like, a complete absence of social amenities, and a comfortless house in which curtains were *taboo* and carpets reduced to a minimum—not because there was no money to buy them, but because the master of the house had an unreasonable terror of fire. In writing of the Brontës it is never wise to stress the bleakness of Haworth, because Charlotte, Emily, and Anne, happened to love it better than any other place in the world. But Miss Branwell was not a Brontë and she did not like Haworth. She did not like its rather grim and unsociable people, and she shivered in the icy blasts that swept round and through the Parsonage in winter from the snowclad moors behind it. But for twenty years she kept up her end gallantly. She brought order and method into a house where both were badly needed. She was always a cheerful companion for Mr. Brontë when he desired company, and ready to argue with him when he wished to argue. To the children she taught such things as she was competent to teach, the elements of learning, household work and, above all, method; and they were not ungrateful for her lessons. But, their tasks once done, she very wisely left them to follow their natural bent, and never attempted to impose herself on them, to dictate their tastes, supervise their games, or pour cold water on their young ambitions. And all the while, by stinting herself, and by wearing out her old caps and gowns, she was saving money out of her very small private income, in order that her nieces might not be penniless, when she and their father were no more. How confidently those nieces counted on her disinterested affection may be judged from a letter of Charlotte's in which, after explaining her reasons for wishing to go to Brussels, she informs her aunt that she will be expected to finance the scheme. The letter is dated 21 September 1841, and the following extract is worth quoting, because it is so typically 'Charlotte':

'I feel certain, while I am writing, that you will see the propriety of what I say; you always like to use your money to the best advantage; you are not fond of making shabby purchases; when you do confer a favour, it is often done in style; and depend upon it, £50 or £100 thus laid out would be well employed. Of course, I know no other friend in the world to whom I could apply on this subject except yourself. I feel an absolute certainty that if this privilege were allowed us, it would be the making of us for life. Papa will perhaps think it a wild ambitious scheme; but who ever rose in the world without ambition? When he left Ireland to go to Cambridge University, he was as ambitious as I am now. I want us *all* to go on. I know we have talents, and I want them to be turned to account. I look to you, aunt, to help us. I think you will not refuse.'

We may hope that the good old lady smiled at the suggestion that she liked doing things in style. Anyhow she duly provided the money. And then, just when increasing years and growing infirmities seemed likely to make her continued presence in the house a burden rather than a blessing, Aunt Branwell died. Her death does not seem to have left any great gap in the lives of the survivors. She had never counted deeply in any of the things in which her nieces were really interested. She was a familiar part of the furniture of life, a link with the past; and the snapping of such links is always painful. But she had ceased to be in any way indispensable; Emily was quite competent to fill her place. Incidentally, her vacant room must have provided a welcome extension of space in those cramped quarters. It meant that the sisters would have a little more elbow-room and that Ellen Nussey could be more suitably entertained when she came to Haworth. To say this is not to charge the Brontës with ingratitude or any lack of proper feeling. After a certain age nobody is indispensable, and his, or her, removal seems only a part of the kindly law of Nature. But in all the pathetic story of Haworth Parsonage Aunt Branwell is surely not the least pathetic figure.

Mr. Brontë was what the Americans would call a more difficult proposition. He believed in himself, he had strong prejudices and several strange obsessions, he was a confirmed hypochondriac, and, though his normal manner was one of old-fashioned courtesy, he was capable of violent explosions. Yet none of the children seems ever to have been in the least afraid of him. They realized, as children are quick to do, that their father's bark was much more formidable than his bite. His daughters were accustomed to his eccentricities and discounted them: they respected his desire for privacy; they never openly challenged his authority or behaved otherwise than dutifully; and in return they enjoyed a large liberty. Mr. Brontë was too selfish a man, and too much absorbed in his own health, to serve as a model to parents; but in his own way he was fond of all his children, and far too indulgent to his only son.

As for Charlotte, she knew her father from A to Z and had learnt in her teens how to manage him. Hers was the master-will in the Parsonage, not because she was in any sense domineering or despotic, but because she was the only member of the family who had a settled policy and the driving force that gets things done. Quiet, persuasive, but persistent, she wore down opposition. Romantic and melodramatic in the world of her own imagination, in the practical affairs of life she was a stern realist. More constantly and more acutely than her sisters she recognized the precariousness of their position. From quite early years she had realized that something must be done to equip them for earning their own livelihood in the only way which was possible for them in those days, namely, by teaching; and it was she who took the initiative in all the plans which were directed towards that end. It was she who sent herself to school again, at Roe Head, in spite of the miserable experiences at Cowan Bridge; she who took Emily

7

back with her to the same establishment, and when that wild spirit began to droop in captivity, substituted the more plastic Anne; she who decided when they should go out as governesses, and who was to stay at home; she who planned and carried through the Brussels adventure, and not only dragged the unhappy Emily with her, but drew her father out of his shell to accompany them. And it was she who dreamed of the joint school which was to keep them always together, for the dearest wish of her heart was that when the inevitable day came and Mr. Brontë died, she and Emily and Anne might somehow not be separated.

But the separation came; not through the death of Mr. Brontë, for he survived them all, but through a rapid succession of stunning and unexpected blows. After his moral collapse and intolerable behaviour, the death of Branwell in September 1848, though it was a severe shock, could not be regarded as a calamity; but when Emily followed him in December, and Anne in the May of 1849, the breach with the past was almost complete and Charlotte was left alone with her father, either to succumb to life or to begin it afresh. It was not in Charlotte's nature to succumb to anything; she had in her little body the stuff of which heroines are made. But the prospect was a terrible one, for Mr. Brontë was too infirm to obtain another *cure*, and too poor to leave Haworth without one, and the new life would have to be built up on the actual ruins of the old, where memory could not be duped, and where every sight and sound, every returning season and scent of moor or meadow, must bring a stab of pain, till time robbed them of their power to hurt.

After burying the last of her sisters at Scarborough and lingering for a few weeks on the Yorkshire coast to recover her emotional balance, if that were possible, Charlotte came home towards the end of June 1849. She had refused the company of Ellen Nussey. For what lay in front of her she needed, not sympathy, but the stark, hard courage which she could only find in herself. She had a brief interview with her father in his study; then she crossed the narrow passage and shut herself alone in the room, more charged for her with poignant memories than any other spot on earth, to endure the worst.

Charlotte endured and triumphed; but the victory was not won easily, and the great dog, half mastiff, half bull-dog, which whined and whimpered every morning at the door of what had once been Emily's bedroom, did not help to make it any easier. Her pen was the weapon with which Charlotte fought her way from something like despair to resignation. The success of her first published novel, *Jane Eyre*, had not only opened up a new sphere of activity, but had brought her new friends and interests, and soon after her return she sat down to pick up the broken threads of *Shirley* and finish a story which had been interrupted by the tragedy of the past few months.

c

What effort of will it must have cost her to detach herself from her surroundings in the very room in which Emily had died in agony, and Anne had faded away, we can only guess; but none can refuse to do homage to that indomitable spirit.

Villette followed *Shirley*, and Charlotte learned how it felt to be a celebrity. She enjoyed her success, but she was too shy to care about the limelight, and too mentally honest ever to get herself out of perspective. She visited London, and had to submit to a little mild lionizing, but she was glad, as the Brontës always were, to get back to Haworth with its moors and its memories. Meanwhile, Mr. Arthur Bell Nicholls, her father's curate, was falling deeply in love with her. There was something about Charlotte, something that does not appear in her portraits, which appealed to the masculine in men. Many people have fallen in love with Emily since her death; alone of the Brontë sisters, Charlotte had lovers in her lifetime. It may be added that, until Mr. Nicholls appeared upon the scene, she had never felt 'any compunctious visitings of nature' in turning them down. He was of her own age: a little too plump perhaps for romance, but quite a presentable man, with a beard, a serious, intelligent face, and kind eyes. That he had enjoyed his portrait in *Shirley* proves that he was neither vain nor without a sense of humour. For the rest he was a thoroughly good man with much delicacy of feeling, deep and lasting affections, and a loyalty which was proof against any tests. He was fully

10

aware of Charlotte's distaste for clergymen in general and for curates in particular; but a man who respects his own calling and is conscious of inward worth and a good outward presence may reasonably hope to overcome such prejudices. Moreover, Mr. Nicholls was 'a somebody' in his own home in Ireland, and free from any kind of inferiority complex. What he did not know, and what none of her contemporaries even guessed, was that the memory of M. Paul Heger stood between Charlotte and any attempt to capture her heart. But, probably, even if he had known it, such knowledge would not have prevented Mr. Nicholls from making the attempt, for he was a very determined man.

Charlotte had become conscious of the interest which her father's curate was taking in her; but she felt little interest in him, and had given him no encouragement—unless it were encouragement to have credited him with *some* good qualities in *Shirley*. It was therefore a most unwelcome surprise for her when one evening after transacting parish business with Mr. Brontë in the study, Mr. Nicholls, instead of leaving the house, came uninvited into the dining-room where she was sitting, and in a voice strangled by emotion blurted out the story of his love. A less ardent flame might well have been quenched by the stream of cold water which Charlotte immediately turned on to it. She had been startled by the intensity of its warmth; but she knew her own mind, and did not hesitate to speak it with her usual candour. In a letter to Ellen Nussey, dated 15 December 1852, she described the scene with a certain cool detachment, and added: 'Attachment to Mr. Nicholls you are aware I have never entertained, but the poignant pity inspired by his state on Monday evening, by the hurried revelation of his feelings for many months, is something galling and irksome to me.' Galling and irksome, because she did not like to be constrained to feel pity for a man in whose company she had 'a sense of incongruity and uncongeniality in feelings, tastes, principles'. Her sense of his uncongeniality was made perfectly clear to Mr. Nicholls, and he went home in a subdued frame of mind, to digest as best he might this unqualified rejection of his suit.

Mr. Brontë would probably have been indignant with anybody who had tried to rob him of his daughter. By all the best standards of the day she was ear-marked as his companion for the remainder of his days. But he was particularly indignant with his curate who had shown himself not only predatory but presumptuous. Charlotte was shocked by the violence of his language. Still, it was good for Mr. Nicholls to know that behind the daughter was an angry and implacable 'Papa'.

So Mr. Nicholls abandoned hope and prepared to leave Haworth; but during the few months which had to elapse before his preparations could be completed he was quite unable to conceal the bitterness of his disappointment and to show a brave face to the world. The poor man did not actually 'sit sighing 'neath a green willow tree', but he lost his appetite, shunned the society of his fellows, and, when seen abroad, had all the appearance of one who has just received a mortal wound. This behaviour made things rather uncomfortable for Charlotte, and in order to avoid unpleasant meetings, she went off on a visit to London. But she was back again in May, and went as usual to Haworth Church on Whit-Sunday, where Mr. Nicholls was to officiate for the last time. This perhaps was not very wise; though it is difficult to see how, being at home, she could have done otherwise, for her truthfulness was of the kind that would not allow her to invent a headache, when she had not got one. Possibly, too, she may have thought that her absence would be taken as a sign of weakness or even of an uneasy conscience. But the sight of her at the communion rails proved too much for Mr. Nicholls. He collapsed completely, and could only finish the service in broken whispers.

Mr. Brontë, when he heard of the scene, was once again very angry: as any father well might be; for Mr. Nicholls had publicly called attention to his daughter in a very marked way, and in a love story the role of the rejected swain is a more sympathetic one than that of the 'cruel fair'. 'Unmanly' was the epithet with which he branded the conduct of his curate. But Charlotte was deeply moved. Mr. Nicholls had, in fact, behaved rather like one of her own more melodramatic heroes; and this did him no harm in her eyes. She certainly began to feel some twinges of remorse.

On the evening of Whit-Monday Mr. Nicholls came to the Parsonage to say good-bye. In a letter to her friend, written immediately afterwards, Charlotte gave a vivid description of this momentous visit. The dining-room was up for cleaning and scrubbing, and consequently Mr. Nicholls did not find her there, when he left her father's study. He supposed that he would have to go away without seeing her, and after hesitating for a few moments, went out of the house. But Charlotte was watching from some post of vantage, and seeing that he lingered long at the gate, she yielded to a sudden impulse, and ran out, trembling and miserable, to speak to him.

'I found him', she wrote, 'standing against the garden door in a paroxysm of anguish, sobbing as women never sob. Of course I went straight to him. Very few words were interchanged, those few barely articulate. Poor fellow! But he wanted such hope and such encouragement as I could not give him. Still I trust he must know now that I am not blind and indifferent to his constancy and grief.'

So Ellen Nussey concluded that, though her friend felt very sorry for the 'poor fellow', her sense of the incompatibility of their feelings, tastes, and principles, remained unshaken, and that the incident was closed. Had she known that some of the 'very few and barely articulate words interchanged' gave permission to Mr. Nicholls to write, and a promise to answer his letters, Ellen might have felt less certain about the finality of the parting.

Why did Charlotte make this vital concession, the first step on the road to surrender? Perhaps it was due to an impulse of purely human sympathy. She knew how it felt to love without hope, to long for some kind of communication, however formal, with the beloved being, to ache for letters that never came. Or perhaps she was already beginning to wonder whether after all she did not like this emotional and devoted man better than she had supposed. In any case, Mr. Nicholls wrote and Charlotte replied, and Mr. Brontë, like Ellen Nussey, remained blissfully ignorant of the correspondence.

In the following September Mr. Nicholls came to stay with a friend in the neighbourhood of Haworth, and it is more than probable that he and Charlotte met once more in secret. In the same September Mrs. Gaskell paid her first visit to the Parsonage. She noted that Charlotte, after conducting her to bed, would return alone to the dining-room and spend long hours pacing up and down the room. Quite naturally Mrs. Gaskell supposed that at such moments her hostess was living again in the past in the room in which she and her sisters had so often walked arm-in-arm round the table, discussing their ambitions, their hopes, and their fears. But it is more likely that

Charlotte was absorbed in the present, wrestling with a problem which was becoming urgent, trying to see clearly into her own mind, weighing pros and cons. For she was soon to make an important decision. Charlotte hated dissimulation, and she felt determined that if her relations with Mr. Nicholls were to continue (and she meant them to continue) there must no longer be any concealment. In January 1854, with her permission, Mr. Nicholls came to Haworth openly and unashamed. Charlotte told her astonished parent of what had been happening, and 'stipulated' (the word is her own) for opportunities of becoming better acquainted with her lover. On this occasion we cannot help feeling a little sympathy with Mr. Brontë. He had been made to look rather foolish. He had been allowed to bark very loud and very fiercely in defence of his daughter, to feel himself a very important and formidable watch-dog; and now, without a word of warning, he was suddenly called off, and bidden to let the intruder pass. There were the customary scenes; but when Charlotte 'stipulated', opposition crumbled, and 'Papa', still growling, came more or less obediently to heel.

By the following April Charlotte had made up her mind. She sent for Mr. Nicholls and dictated the terms on which she was prepared to surrender. He was to return to Haworth as Mr. Brontë's curate and live at the Parsonage. Charlotte would not be separated from her father. The little dark room on the ground floor, which had hitherto been used as a place for storing wood, would be converted into a second study, and Mr. Brontë would still be (nominally at all events) master in his own house. Mr. Nicholls was not to carry off his bride; his bride was to carry off him. The terms, in short, were a compromise very favourable to the Brontës, but Mr. Nicholls accepted them without demur and probably with alacrity.

It is reasonably certain that, when she married him, Charlotte was not in love with her husband. But she was a practical woman and 38 years old. The problem which had always haunted her still remained unsolved, namely, what was to become of her when Mr. Brontë died. For fame had not yet brought her a fortune, and the £500 a-piece which she had received for her three novels did not even provide a competence. Her health was always precarious, and she may well have wondered whether she would be able permanently to support herself by her pen. By marrying Mr. Nicholls she might have to sacrifice some of her literary ambitions, but in return she would win to safety. If she did not actually love him, she had at least learned to like and respect him, and in providing for herself she was also providing for her father. Perhaps her long hesitation was chiefly due to a reluctance to part with her complete freedom of action. It had always been irksome to her to be at anybody's beck and call. Probably, too, she had realized that with an emotional temperament Mr. Nicholls combined a firm and determined will, and she may have feared that it would sometimes clash with her own. But she could trust in an affection which had been so long and severely tried; and, for her own part, she was resolved to do her duty loyally as a wife, who no longer belongs entirely to herself.

It was left to Charlotte to inform Mr. Brontë of what had been settled for him. As was to be expected he made a great to-do, and, as was equally to be expected, when he was tired of protesting, he accepted the inevitable. After all, the arrangements were very much to his advantage; he kept his daughter and secured the permanent services of a curate who had proved his efficiency and was liked in the parish.

The wedding, which by Charlotte's desire was kept very private, took place in Haworth Church at 8 o'clock on the morning of 29 June 1854. At the last moment 'Papa' had a foolish and futile relapse. He refused to go to church; so they went there without him, and Miss Wooler gave away the bride. But it was the old man's last recorded bark. He was glad enough to welcome the couple home from their honeymoon in Ireland, and for the rest of his life he fed tamely, and even gratefully, out of the hand of his son-in-law.

Charlotte's health had improved considerably since her marriage, life was running smoothly at the Parsonage, and although there were far more claims on her time than before, she had started on another novel. After many storms she seemed to have reached calm waters. But the Fate which pursued the Brontës so relentlessly now claimed its last victim, and nine months after her wedding Charlotte was carried to her grave. Early in the new year she had caught a chill, and in February she was obliged to take to her bed with other, and more alarming, symptoms—perpetual nausea, a loathing of all food, and a constant feeling of faintness. These symptoms the local doctor put down to the early stages of pregnancy, and his opinion was confirmed by the best available advice, called in from Bradford. Much anxiety was felt, but no real alarm, till very shortly before the end. It was always hoped that the distressing symptoms would pass away of themselves in the natural course of events. But her strength, though not her will to live, ebbed slowly away and she died, apparently of exhaustion, on 31 March 1855, aged 39 years.

Mr. Nicholls bore his sorrow with great dignity and courage. In granting him his wish Fate had reserved for him a grimly ironical sequel. He had lost the wife to whom he was passionately devoted and for whom he had sacrificed his independence, and he was left instead with her father, a man whom he might pity profoundly, but could hardly be expected to revere. But he did not shirk his responsibilities. For nearly six years he lived on in that desolate house, faithful in the discharge of his parochial duties, and unfailingly kind to Mr. Brontë, now increasingly infirm, and nearly blind.

He never sought publicity for himself as the husband of Charlotte Brontë, and as steadily refused to furnish 'copy' about her to the merely curious; but whenever her fairness or her accuracy was challenged, he rushed to her defence with a warmth which was sometimes more chivalrous than convincing. When at last Mr. Brontë died in 1861, Mr. Nicholls returned to his home at Banagra, in King's County, Ireland, where he had property, took to farming, married a cousin, and died at the advanced age of 90 in 1906.

In spite of his many admirable qualities of heart and head, Mr. Nicholls never succeeded in winning the approbation of Miss Nussey, and for that reason probably has never enjoyed 'a good press'. Spinster ladies are apt to look with an unfriendly eye on the husbands of their bosom friends. A woman instinctively desires to be first with those whom she loves best, and Ellen Nussey had made a special cult of Charlotte. The match was not of her making; she had not even been allowed to keep pace with the changes in her friend's feelings towards the once-despised curate, and she was reluctant to believe that they had really changed. Probably she resented Mr. Nicholls's wise refusal to allow his wife to visit her in an infected house, and his equally reasonable attempt to secure from her a promise that she would in future burn Charlotte's letters, as soon as read, whenever these contained any glaring indiscretion. Perhaps, too, she thought that with greater care and better nursing her friend need not have died. Somehow she must have managed to make herself disagreeable at the time of Charlotte's death, for the friendly *My dear Miss Nussey . . . very sincerely yours* of Mr. Nicholls's earlier letters changed abruptly to the formal *Dear Madam . . . yours faithfully*, and he was not the man to cool suddenly towards his wife's oldest friend without provocation.

But even if there had been no Ellen Nussey to belittle him, I am afraid that Mr. Nicholls would never have been a popular figure with those ardent souls who look to the Brontës for the perfect embodiment of a high romance. That Charlotte, proud and gifted Charlotte, with her unacknowledged passion for M. Heger and her contempt for curates, should marry one of the latter and be happy with him—this was a tame ending to a romantic story; and there is a predisposition in many minds to believe that the marriage was a regrettable and regretted blunder. And it must be admitted that, from the purely dramatic point of view, the marriage was something of an anti-climax. Yet to anybody whose mind is open to conviction Charlotte's last letters leave little room for doubt that she found in her short married life, not only that feeling of security for which she had always longed, but a new, and perhaps unexpected, happiness in a warm and ever-growing affection for Mr. Nicholls. They were soon on intimate, and even chaffing, terms. She liked his relations, she liked his sermons, she enjoyed his popularity in

Haworth, she even enjoyed his occasional assumptions of authority. To Mrs. Gaskell she wrote: 'I have a good, kind, attached husband, and every day my own attachment to him grows stronger.' In her correspondence with Ellen Nussey, 'Mr. Nicholls' or 'my husband', soon becomes 'Arthur', and finally 'my dear boy'—and this in a letter which begins with an expression of strong distaste for any exaggeration in the language of the feelings. In those nine months Charlotte certainly learned to love, as well as respect, her husband; and when, still clinging desperately to life, she read her doom in his anguished eyes, she murmured 'I am not going to die, am I? He will not separate us; we have been so happy.'

In a matter of this kind it is wise not to try to know better than Charlotte herself.

2. *Emily Brontë*

IT is perhaps easier for the imaginative bio-grapher to write about Emily Brontë than about almost any other literary celebrity, for the simple reason that so little is known about her, and he is therefore able to re-create her in his own image, or in any other image that he may happen to prefer. More than one such writer has of late taken full advantage of this fair opportunity for conjecture, even to the length of finding in her greatest poem, *No Coward Soul is Mine*, 'Satan's hymn to God!' It may be well, therefore, to get back for a moment to the hard facts which underlie the problem of that strangely arresting personality.

Next to her genius, the most astonishing thing about Emily Brontë is the silence which sur-rounds her life. Charlotte and Branwell both made friends who kept their letters and treasured their sayings; Anne won the affection of her pupils and employers; but Emily made no friends, and shunned acquaintances. Even in the intimacy of the family circle she kept back a large part of her-self. When she was dead and famous, those who had known her searched their memories for reveal-ing traits, and found, possibly to their own surprise and certainly to our loss, that they could remember nothing that was really worth remembering. She was taller than her sisters; she lived on porridge and milk-puddings; she played the piano; she did the house-work and helped in the kitchen; she was fond of dogs; she walked on the moors—and that was generally all. Long after Charlotte's death, Miss Ellen Nussey, who had enjoyed special opportunities, revived the memories of her first visit to Haworth in 1833. She was writing to a literary acquaintance about her famous literary friends, and she strove to be worthy of the occasion. Whenever Ellen Nussey tried to write worthily of her famous literary friends, her style and diction are rather wonderful; but she comes nearer than anybody else to telling us something significant about Emily at the age of 15. She describes her as having a 'lithesome, graceful figure', naturally beautiful hair, unbecomingly worn, 'no complexion', and 'kind, kindling eyes', which were sometimes dark grey, and at others dark blue; 'but she did not often look at you: she was too reserved.' Then Miss Nussey continues:

'In fine, suitable weather delightful rambles were made over the moors, and down into glens and ravines that here and there broke the monotony of the moorland. The rugged bank and rippling brook were treasures of delight. Emily, Anne, and Branwell used to ford the streams and sometimes placed stepping stones for the other two. There was always a lingering delight in these sports. . . . Emily especially had a gleesome delight in these nooks of beauty—her reserve for the time vanished.'

'One long ramble in those early days' had brought the party to a remote spot 'familiar to

Emily and Anne, which they called "the Meeting of the Waters" '.

'Seated here, we were hidden from all the world, nothing appearing in view but miles and miles of heather, a glorious blue sky, and brightening sun. A fresh breeze wafted on us its exhilarating radiance; we laughed, and made mirth of each other, and settled we would call ourselves the quartette. Emily, half-reclining on a slab of stone, played like a young child with the tadpoles in the water, making them swim about, and then fell to moralizing on the strong and the weak, the brave and the cowardly, as she chased them with her hand. No serious cloud of sorrow had so far cast its gloom on nature's youth and buoyancy, and nature's simplest offerings were fountains of pleasure and enjoyment.'

Thus Ellen Nussey; and because of the beautiful, kindling, dark-grey, dark-blue eyes, because, too, she was said to have been a pretty baby, and because it would heighten the pathos of her early death, some sentimental writers have persuaded themselves that Emily Brontë was beautiful. It would be unfair to judge of her appearance from existing portraits. No beauty, however brilliant, could have survived the ordeal of being painted by Branwell. But none of her contemporaries found Emily beautiful or even attractive. If they had, they would certainly have said so. We should probably have thought her ugly—at all events at first sight. The Brontë nose did not make for beauty. As for the reserve which Miss Nussey noted as a salient characteristic at fifteen, it grew with years into an almost impenetrable aloofness.

Did Anne ever penetrate behind it and read her sister's soul? It is impossible to say, for Anne died within a few months of Emily, leaving no records except her simple poems and her two novels. Ellen Nussey says that in their childhood the two youngest of the Brontë girls were like twins, always together and always in harmony. They had collaborated over the Gondal stories, and paced arm-in-arm round the parlour table. Probably Anne understood her sister's moods better than anybody else; but it is difficult to believe that she could have sympathized with, or even understood, that sister's deepest and most daring thoughts. Their minds were cast in very different moulds. At all events, in her last, grim, obstinate struggle with death, Emily held both her sisters at arm's length, and wrung their hearts by refusing to accept their aid or sympathy.

As for Charlotte, it was not till 1845, when she discovered the little washing-book, in which Emily's poems were written in a microscopic hand, and took the liberty (fiercely resented by the owner) of reading them, that she even guessed the depths which lay behind her sister's reserve. From that moment her sisterly affection was tinged with feelings both of admiration and remorse—remorse for her failure to appreciate Emily at her true value and win her confidence. She tried hard to bridge the gulf which time and habit had dug between them, and of which she herself was now acutely conscious. But it was too late. In December of

1848 Emily passed for ever beyond her reach. 'Death stepped tacitly and took her', and Charlotte's grief was all the more poignant, because it was so full of 'might-have-beens'.

That is the impression which one receives from Charlotte's letters at this period. But it seems more than doubtful whether the 'might-have-beens' could ever have been realized. Charlotte was, though she did not know it, just the kind of elder sister to whom a rather shy and sensitive genius could never have opened its secret doors—practical, critical, and quietly, kindly, but persistently, dominating. She and Emily could never have been kindred spirits. Their minds and imaginations moved on different planes. With all her insight into character, Charlotte could never have understood, or entered into, the poetic temperament of her sister.

So Emily Brontë died at the age of 30, an enigma in her own generation and in her father's house, and all that we really know about her inner life and thoughts is contained in her writings—some poems and a single novel. We may be quite sure that she did not reveal the whole of herself in what she wrote, and reasonably sure that she did not always herself understand whither the spirit was driving her. We cannot reconstruct her as she was, from the glimpses which she gives us into the workings of her mind; but we can at least draw certain inferences which help to explain both her reserve and the nature and quality of her work.

All children, when they are thrown much upon their own resources, create for themselves an imaginary world which becomes as real as, and far more exciting than, the actual facts of everyday existence. The Brontë children were thrown much upon their own resources, and the happiest hours of their childhood were spent in dreaming dreams. For most people this imaginary world fades into the distance with adolescence, partly because the wings of their imagination are incapable of further expansion, and partly because their everyday life becomes either too full or too absorbing to leave time for dreams. But Emily was a poet, and her wings continued to expand. For her, the life of the imagination remained the most real, and the only truly satisfying, part of existence. She could feel significance and beauty (on the moors, for example) with an intensity which was rapture; and, what was peculiarly characteristic of herself, she continued to feel them in those vague, but passionate, yearnings which are the experience of childhood. Two things seem to stand out clearly from her poetry.

(1) She was conscious of a sense of loneliness, sometimes terrifying, and sometimes exhilarating; terrifying, when it made the world seem bleak and empty; exhilarating, when it made her feel in harmony with the elemental forces of Nature.

(2) She had a craving for some absorbing kind of love, of which possession was the essence, though the body counted for little in it—a love that was at once passionate and sexless.

But Emily did not only dream; she thought, and she had a powerful and original mind. We do not know how much she read of contemporary poetry—probably not much. But she must almost certainly have been familiar with *Adonais*. Here is Shelley:

> He is made one with Nature: there is heard
> His voice in all her music, from the moan
> Of thunder to the song of night's sweet bird;
> He is a presence to be felt and known
> In darkness and in light, from herb and stone,
> Spreading itself where'er that Power may move
> Which has withdrawn his being to its own:
> Which wields the world with never wearied love,
> Sustains it from beneath, and kindles it above.

And here is Emily Brontë:

(a)

> And thou art now a Spirit pouring
>   Thy presence into all:
> The essence of the tempest's roaring,
>   And of the tempest's fall.

(b)

> With wide-embracing love
> Thy spirit animates eternal years,
>   Pervades and broods above,
> Changes, sustains, dissolves, creates, and rears.

The plagiarism was no doubt unconscious; but the resemblance is almost too great to be a mere coincidence. Possibly Branwell had recited the lines to his sisters, and Emily had assimilated them.

He seems to have been fond of spouting Shelley. Be that as it may, *No Coward Soul is Mine* is a great intellectual, as well as a great spiritual, achievement.

And that was the trouble. The inner life of Emily Brontë, the thoughts which she thought and the dreams which she dreamed, had no relevance to 'that state of life into which it had pleased God to call her'. This was true to some extent of Charlotte also; but it was much harder for Emily to adjust herself to the claims of real life, because she lacked some of those normal sympathies and affections which help to make life interesting. She could feel significance and beauty in the wildest forms of Nature, but not in the lives, loves, joys, and sorrows of those amongst whom her lot was cast. She was fond of animals, but not of children. She did not care for people. She had no curiosity to enter into and explore their minds; and her own she instinctively bolted and barred in their presence. She was more alone in company than in a solitude which she could people with her fancies, and only on the moors did she feel herself wholly in communion with something outside herself.

Such a clash between the demands of the inner self and the claims of life would, in many, have ended in revolt. But Emily Brontë was no rebel. Grimly and stoically she accepted the facts of life, and to the daughters of the Rev. Patrick Brontë, until the publication of their novels in 1847 had opened up new vistas, the facts of life meant the ultimate choice between a situation as governess in a private house and teaching in a school. Sooner or later—and it always seemed likely to be sooner rather than later—Mr. Brontë must die. There would no longer be a home at Haworth or anywhere else, and they would all have to earn their daily bread. To be prepared for the inevitable, to acquire useful knowledge in order to be able to impart it to others—that was the plain duty which the Brontë girls felt to be imposed upon them by the circumstances of their life. For Emily it involved a very stern self-discipline. She must sacrifice the life of the imagination with its fearful joys and 'rapturous anguish', and learn to live 'without the aid of joy'. She tried; but, courageous though she was both physically and morally, it is interesting to note that she twice had to admit defeat. The first occasion was when, at the age of seventeen, she accompanied Charlotte to Roe Head (a particularly friendly, cheerful and happy school), pined for three months, like a wild bird in a cage, and had to be sent home. The second, when, three years later, she went as mistress to Law Hill School, Southowram, near Halifax, and resigned her post after six unhappy months. Whilst there was still a home at Haworth, Emily could not live anywhere else. But the future must have looked very dark for her, for the pathetically futile idea that the three sisters, without adequate capital, could set up a school of their own, could only have been envisaged by her as a mitigated form of bondage. In this connexion Charlotte wrote to M. Heger: 'Émilie n'aime pas beaucoup l'instruction, mais elle s'occuperait du ménage, et quoiqu'un peu recluse, elle a trop bon cœur pour ne pas faire son possible pour les enfants.'

Thus far Emily Brontë seems to explain herself. But there is one poem which, if it is really autobiographical, would make nonsense of the foregoing analysis of her character. Familiar as the lines are, they must be quoted in full.

Cold in the earth—and the deep snow piled above thee,
    Far, far removed, cold in the dreary grave,
Have I forgot, my only Love, to love thee,
    Severed at last by Time's all-severing wave?

Now, when alone, do my thoughts no longer hover
    Over the mountains on that northern shore,
Resting their wings where heath and fern-leaves cover
    Thy noble heart for ever, evermore?

Cold in the earth—and fifteen wild Decembers
    From those brown hills have melted into spring;
Faithful indeed is the spirit that remembers
    After such years of change and suffering.

Sweet Love of youth, forgive, if I forget thee,
    While the world's tide is bearing me along,
Other desires and other hopes beset me,
    Hopes which obscure, but cannot do thee wrong.

No later light has lightened up my heaven,
    No second morn has ever shone for me;
All my life's bliss from thy dear life was given,
    All my life's bliss is in the grave with thee.

But when the days of golden dreams had perished,
  And even Despair was powerless to destroy,
Then did I learn how existence could be cherished,
  Strengthened and fed, without the aid of joy.

Then did I check the tears of useless passion.
  Weaned my young soul from yearning after thine,
Sternly denied its burning wish to hasten
  Down to that tomb already more than mine.

And even yet I dare not let it languish,
  Dare not indulge in memory's rapturous pain,
Once drinking deep of that divinest anguish,
  How could I seek the empty world again?

Most people, apparently, take this poem literally, and believe that, at one period of her life, Emily was passionately in love with somebody whose identity has never been divulged. The lines must almost certainly have been composed in Brussels, when she was twenty-four, for at no other time was Emily far away (as the poem implies) from 'that northern shore' and its beloved mountains. The theme, it should be noticed, is fidelity to a first and only Love *after a long lapse of years*— 'fifteen wild Decembers'. We need not be pedantic about the number '15'. But if 'severed at last by Time's all-severing wave', and 'after such years of change and suffering', mean anything, they mean a substantial period of time, and any substantial period of time that we may fix on takes Emily back to her early teens. But apart from this, is it credible that, if there had been any love story in her life, Emily, most reticent and reserved of

F

women, would have published to the world a secret so intimate and so sacred, even under an assumed name? That there is passion in the poem, nobody will deny. But Emily was a poet, and poets can feel passionately about imagined experiences, as well as about their contacts with real life. If they did not, Tennyson (to take one instance only) could never have written *Maud*. There is passion and romance in *Maud*, yet in his actual relations with women Tennyson was never either passionate or romantic. It seems reasonable, therefore, to suppose, though Romance would wish it otherwise, that this poem is true only of that imaginary world in which Emily lived her happiest and also her most poignant hours, and still to see her, as she appeared to her contemporaries, unapproachable by mortal man.

For those who live by the imagination, and find the real world empty of delight, there is a supreme joy in filling its emptiness with the creations of their own brain. Emily must have known this joy when she was writing *Wuthering Heights*. Yet judged by any ordinary standards, she was singularly ill-equipped for the task of novel-writing. Charlotte, from the age of 5, had been a critical, and rather censorious, student of character, but Emily's acquaintance with human nature, as it existed outside herself, was of the slightest. She did not even know the people in her own parish. She had heard them talk, and she had listened to her father's strange stories about them—which must have suggested the prevalence of a harsh brutality—but she had never tried to enter into their lives. 'My sister's disposition', wrote Charlotte in the preface to a second edition of *Wuthering Heights*, 'was not naturally gregarious; circumstances favoured and fostered her tendency to seclusion; except to go to church or take a walk on the hills, she seldom crossed the threshold of home. Though her feeling for the people round was benevolent, intercourse with them was never sought; nor, with very few exceptions, ever experienced.'

Nelly Dean is, no doubt, a more or less faithful portrait of Tabby Brown, the devoted friend and servant at the Parsonage, but for the other characters in her story Emily had to draw upon her own imaginative experiences of life, which is a very different thing from 'holding up the mirror to Nature'. Most of her characters have the unreasoned loves, hates and cruelty of children, and in Heathcliff are incarnate the loneliness and the yearning for a passionate yet almost sexless love which haunt her poetry. At any moment the story might become ridiculous; but there is a strange power behind it, which makes it always fascinating and sometimes terrifying. In hardly any other book are we so constantly aware of genius, for we see it continually at work transforming the potentially absurd into the poignant or the horrible. And the effect is immensely heightened by Emily's gift for creating atmosphere and background—an atmosphere in which we cease to ask, 'Is this possible?' It matters not what house is the original of Wuthering Heights; we know the place in all its moods as well as we know our own home; and what Emily felt about the moors she has conveyed to us in a prose which, at its best, is unsurpassed in its effortless beauty.

If the 'Dear Sir' of Mr. Newby's letter, found in the rosewood desk which was once Emily's, was addressed to Ellis and not to Acton Bell (which seems unlikely), Emily had contemplated a second novel. One would guess *a priori* that she could only have repeated the Heathcliff theme in a different and, probably, a less convincing form. But it is of the essence of genius to confound the wise. As a poet, certainly, she still had much to say. The range of her genius had its obvious limits, but within those limits what might she not have achieved!

3. Brontë Legends

UNDER a glass case at Haworth Parsonage, in the little narrow room over the hall, which was once Emily Brontë's bedroom, there is[1] a comb with charred teeth. To the untrained eye it has all the appearance of being a dog-comb; but a label informs the curious that this was Emily Brontë's comb, and that there is a story attached to it. Rumour has it that five other combs with charred teeth were aspirants for the honour of admission to the glass case. If this be true (I cannot vouch for its truth) and if any one of the five was less suggestive of the kennel, it seems a pity that the story could not have been attached to *it*; for the Brontë sisters were fastidious people and liked pretty things.

It is highly improbable that there would be any comb with charred teeth under a glass case in Haworth Parsonage to-day if it had not been for Miss A. Mary F. Robinson, the most gifted and persuasive of all the creators or purveyors of Brontë legends. Miss Robinson wrote her *Emily Brontë* for the 'Eminent Women Series' in 1883, and her book may be said to have started that quest of the 'real Emily', which has since led imaginative writers to discover in the most elusive of the

[1] Or was in April 1930. The small rooms of the Parsonage are now so filled with glass cases that they have ceased to look like living rooms, and it is difficult to realize that anything ever happened in them.

37

Brontë sisters either a kindred spirit or a being of almost superhuman proportions. Perhaps in some cases the two points of view are not always incompatible. Nobody will for a moment dispute Emily's claim to be called eminent; the main difficulty of her biographers lies in the fact that, apart from her published works, hardly anything is known about her. So Miss Robinson was set the arduous task of making literary bricks with a minimum of straw. Some of the bricks she made are pretty bricks; but they are not always good history, and when subjected to the customary processes of criticism, they have a way of crumbling into poetic dust.

As a biographer Miss Robinson had two weaknesses. In the first place she sometimes embroiders a doubtful tale, already told by somebody else, with matter of her own invention, the purpose of such embroidery being, apparently, to keep her narrative at a high level of pathos. Mrs. Gaskell, for instance, who was not always critical of her authorities and who was apt to attach an exaggerated value to local gossip, had told a story about a dress which had been given to Mrs. Brontë by a friend, but never worn. This dress Mr. Brontë discovered one day in a drawer in his wife's room, and cut into strips, she, be it noted, being out of the room at the time. There may be some truth in the story, as Mr. Brontë was absurdly nervous about fire, and the inmates of the Parsonage were not allowed to wear dresses of what he regarded as dangerously inflammable material.[1] But Miss Robinson makes the story more poignant by saying that the dress was Mrs. Brontë's 'favourite dress', that its destruction took place before her very eyes, and that Mr. Brontë destroyed it because he was too proud to allow his wife to accept gifts of wearing apparel from anybody but himself.

And there is another very tall story (told to Mrs. Gaskell by the woman who had nursed Mrs. Brontë in her last illness) of six little pairs of coloured boots warming in front of the kitchen fire for six little pairs of feet sent out, unattended and in uncertain weather, to ramble over the lonely moors; which boots Mr. Brontë, when nobody was looking, threw into the fire, because he disliked coloured boots. Mrs. Gaskell seems not to have made the simple calculation that at the time of the story (1820) the ages of the six gallant little pedestrians must have ranged upwards from one and a bit to eight. Miss Robinson accepts the story and adds that Mrs. Brontë had to see her children's boots reduced to cinders, 'when she had no money in her pocket to get new ones'. We wonder how Miss Robinson knew this.

In the second place, she occasionally makes large assumptions and treats them as established facts, without warning her readers that she has strayed into the realm of pure speculation. This is noticeably the case in the emotional and rather rhetorical passages in which she dwells

[1] Ellen Nussey was informed of this on her first visit to Haworth.

on the affection felt by Emily for her brother Branwell. Branwell died in the September of 1848;
Emily's death in the following December came as
an unexpected and crushing blow to her family.
According to Charlotte it was precipitated by
Emily's refusal to take any ordinary precautions
when she fell ill soon after Branwell's funeral.
Emily did not believe in doctors and refused point
blank to see one. Up to the eleventh hour she
would not even admit that she was ill, would not
forgo one of her daily occupations, would not
listen to advice, would not allow the subject of her
health to be mentioned in her presence. Most of
us know people who behave in a similar way when
they are ill, and we do not count it to them for
righteousness. We cannot help being awed by the
almost superhuman courage and strength of will
which enabled Emily to come downstairs, unaided,
to the sitting-room and take up her sewing, when
she was actually in the first stages of her death
agony. But that kind of obstinacy, born of pride,
is a flaw in character, not a grace. In Emily's case
it did nobody any good and only made her sisters
miserably unhappy. Perhaps Miss Robinson felt
this. At all events she was convinced that her
heroine's refusal to be nursed must have had its
roots in some gentler feeling than an obstinate
pride in self. Miss Robinson found the cause in
a broken heart. So we get a moving picture of
Emily as the patient, tender, devoted sister, waiting
and watching through the lonely night for her

brother's return from the Black Bull, helping him upstairs to bed, protecting him against himself. After dealing faithfully with Branwell's vices, Miss Robinson enters impressively upon her theme.

'But there was one woman's heart strong enough in its compassion to bear the daily disgusts, weaknesses, sins of Branwell's life, and yet persist in aid and affection. She never wavered in her kindness. In that silent house it was the silent Emily who had ever a cheering word for Branwell; it was Emily who still remembered that he was her brother, without that remembrance forcing her heart to numbness. She still hoped to win him back by love.'

And so, when Branwell died unreclaimed, 'she who so mourned her brother' made haste to join him. 'The motive of her life seemed gone.'

Now all this is very moving, but it is pure conjecture and not very plausible conjecture. For, in a letter to Ellen Nussey, written on 3 March 1846 on her return home after a visit to her friend, Charlotte had said:[1]

'My fears [about Branwell] were not in vain. I hear [from Emily] that he had got a sovereign from papa, while I have been away, under pretence of paying a pressing bill; he went immediately and changed it at a public house, and has employed it as was to be expected. Emily concluded her account by saying *"he is a hopeless being"*;[2] it is too true.'

If Emily regarded her brother as 'a hopeless

[1] Mrs. Gaskell quoted this letter in her life of Charlotte, but substituted asterisks for the name of 'Emily', which may have misled Miss Robinson.

[2] The italics are my own.

being' in March 1846, he certainly did not do anything in the course of the next two years which was
likely to make her change her mind. Of course a
single expression of opinion is insufficient proof of
a permanent attitude of mind. But Charlotte, who
mentions her father's overwhelming grief for his
only son, does not even hint that it was shared by
Emily. Moreover, Anne had written *The Tenant of
Wildfell Hall* with Branwell consciously in her
mind. As Anne was certainly devoted to Emily
she would hardly have written and published a
book so calculated to give pain to her sister, if
Emily had really been as deeply attached to Branwell as Miss Robinson supposed. Indeed, Charlotte's letters give the impression that, except by
Mr. Brontë, Branwell's death, after the first shock,
was felt as something of a relief. We have fair
grounds therefore for supposing that Emily shared
her sister's contempt for their wastrel of a brother,
though perhaps with less bitterness, in proportion
as she was less eager to convert the Parsonage into
a school for girls—a project which Branwell's
presence and behaviour had made impossible.

The death of Emily brings us back to the comb
with the charred teeth, for its story is connected
with her last hours. This is briefly what is stated
to have happened. On the morning of her death
Emily insisted on getting up at her usual hour and
dressing herself. But they lit a fire for her and
she sat down on the floor in front of it to comb
her hair. The comb, however, fell from her feeble

hand into the glowing cinders and lay there slowly burning till a servant, attracted by the smell, came into the room. Emily, pointing to the hearth, said: 'My comb is down there; I was too weak to stoop and pick it up.'

We may here note four things about this story. (1) Charlotte did not mention the incident in her letters nor in conversation to Mrs. Gaskell when that lady visited Haworth in September 1853 and heard some particulars of Emily's death. (2) Neither did the servant, Martha Brown, who gave Mrs. Gaskell an account of Emily's death, say anything about the comb. (3) It is extremely unlikely that any other servant was in the Parsonage at the time of the alleged occurrence. (4) As Emily insisted almost to the last that she was not ill, was too proud to accept any assistance in dressing and came downstairs immediately afterwards alone and unaided, it is equally unlikely that she would have said to anybody 'I am too weak to stoop and pick it up'.

The silence of Charlotte and Mrs. Gaskell, significant though it is, and the improbability of the words put into Emily's mouth, would not necessarily be conclusive, if Miss Robinson had produced any substantial evidence in support of her story. But she did not do so, and, to make matters worse, there is a serious flaw in her narrative, which she seems to have overlooked. There is no uncertainty as to which was Emily's bedroom. It is identified by a letter of Charlotte's, written to

Mr. Williams after her sister's death, in which she tells how the dog, *Keeper*, would come and snuffle every morning 'under the door of Emily's little room'. The only room to which Charlotte could have applied the epithet 'little' is the one immediately over the narrow hall, once known as 'the children's study', and, as Mrs. Gaskell noted, there was no fire-place in it. Indeed, owing to the structure of the house, there never could have been a fire-place in that room.

Miss Robinson does not deal with this difficulty and concludes her story by saying 'I have seen the old, broken comb with a large piece burned out of it, and I thought it, I own, more pathetic than the bones of the eleven thousand virgins at Cologne'.

I am not in a position to question the authenticity of the bones of the eleven thousand virgins, but I venture to suggest that Miss Robinson would have been more accurate if she had said '*a* comb', instead of '*the* comb'.

But the most wonderful story of all is the story of the fire. Miss Robinson introduces it with one of her most solemn preludes. 'As time went on and Branwell grew worse and wilder, it was well for the lonely watcher [Emily] that she was strong.' She then continues: 'One night, their father and Branwell being in bed, the girls came upstairs to sleep. Emily had gone on first into the little passage room where she slept, when Charlotte, *passing Branwell's partly opened door,*[1] saw a strange

[1] The italics throughout this story are my own.

bright flare inside.' Whereupon she gave a cry of alarm.

We must pause here to make certain observations.

(1) Where there is fire there is smoke, and through *the partly opened door* it must have poured on to the landing. The girls could not fail to smell it.

(2) Unless he was sleeping with his father (and this is ruled out by the story) Charlotte could not have passed Branwell's room in going to her own. She and Anne slept in the room on the right of Emily's; Mr. Brontë in the room on the left. The only other room which Branwell could have occupied was the one which he used as his studio. This was *behind* the sisters as they came up the stairs on to the landing and passed to their rooms. Unless she had eyes in the back of her head, Charlotte could not have seen into it without turning completely round.

(3) 'As Branwell grew worse and wilder' (if not before) he slept in his father's room. Even if we had not been told this by Mrs. Gaskell we might have guessed it; for Mr. Brontë with his dread of fire would never have allowed his drunken son to sleep alone in a room with a lighted candle.

But to continue the story: On hearing Charlotte's cry, 'Emily came out of her room and, remembering her father's terror of fire, put a warning finger to her lips'. She then bounded down the stairs to fetch the two buckets which were filled with water

45

every night and placed in the kitchen passage near the foot of the stairs, in case of an emergency. She returned with a pail in each hand and 'entered *the blazing room*'—only to discover that it was not the room which was blazing, but the bed, and not so much the bed as the bedding. 'Fortunately the flame had not caught the woodwork. Drunken Branwell, turning in bed, must have *upset the light on to the sheets, for they and the bed were all on fire.*' The contents of the two pails extinguished this fierce blaze and 'Emily came out white and with singed clothes'. Strange to say, like Shadrach, Meshach, and Abednego, Branwell, who was in the very centre of this burning fiery furnace, came out of it unscathed. Even the water seems to have spared him, for Emily carried him in her strong arms to her room and laid him in her own bed to finish his unbroken and drunken sleep.

But first she had to calm 'the three *hysterical* girls' who were huddled together on the landing. The three hysterical girls were Charlotte, Anne, and a young servant, unnamed. The 'young servant' is an unknown quantity; but all the Brontë sisters met death with a calm courage, and it is impossible to believe that any of them would ever have had hysterics in the face of danger. Indeed, this attempt to exalt Emily at the expense of her sisters is a serious flaw in the biography. As for Mr. Brontë, nervous man though he was, he slept peacefully through all the noise and hysterics which were going on just outside his door. Miss Robinson winds up her story by adding, 'Where Emily slept herself that night no one remembers now'. Neither Charlotte nor Mrs. Gaskell throws any light upon this point. They do not even mention the fire. Perhaps it originated in the brain of somebody who thought that Charlotte could not have described the fire in *Jane Eyre* unless she had seen something like it with her own eyes.

Miss Robinson did much to secure for Emily the recognition due to her as a woman of genius. It is a pity, therefore, that she was so little critical of legend and so much inclined to indulge a vivid imagination. In this respect she has been followed by other writers on Emily, but in their way they are often good psychologists. They know what they would like to believe, and what other people would like to believe, and they give it with a conviction and an earnestness which disarm suspicion.

Poor Branwell is a less tempting theme for legend, but, being the brother of Charlotte and of Emily, he could not sink into the oblivion which, when Fate is kind, is the lot of the weak, the mean, the selfish, and the mendacious. Some of his personal friends seem to have been vexed that the women of the family should carry off all the honours, and championed his claim to a share in them. Others of a later generation have felt convinced that a member of so gifted a family must himself have had some spark of genius. His upbringing too was of the kind which, according to the best modern theories, was calculated to produce the rarest fruit. He was never thwarted, he was never harried by discipline, he was never crushed by harsh and unintelligent schoolmasters, or by the ridicule of still harsher schoolfellows. But all that can be said of Branwell is that, if there ever was any spark in him, this particular kind of education managed to extinguish it. He has left nothing of his own, whether in prose or verse, which rises above mediocrity, and, in the face of Charlotte's testimony and the strongest internal evidence, the attempt to connect him in any way with the authorship of *Wuthering Heights* is a forlorn hope.[1] It seems almost strange that none of his supporters has tried to credit him with at least a hand in Emily's great poem *No coward soul is mine*; for it did not appear in the first volume published by the three sisters, it might quite easily have been found in his pockets (after his death) with the love-letters

[1] Mr. E. F. Benson in his *Life of Charlotte Brontë* is less sceptical on this point. But (1) the opening of the story, with which he credits Branwell, is based, as Miss Romer Wilson has shown, on a tale by Hoffmann, and though we know that Emily had read Hoffmann at Brussels, there is no reason for supposing that Branwell was acquainted with that writer. (2) As Emily's ideas of how men talked must have been derived largely from her brother's conversation, it is not surprising to find Mr. Lockwood talking at times like Branwell; nor is it strange (to me at all events) that at the close of the book she should not have troubled to be consistent, and should have used her narrator as a mouthpiece for her own sentiments. (3) Flaws in the construction of a first novel are nothing unusual, and loose threads mean little. (4) The memory of Branwell's friends could be strangely inaccurate; Grundy, for example, who claimed to know the Brontë sisters, thought that they had red hair.

of the lady of Thorpe Green; and did he not stand up in his bed to die? *Q. E. D.* What share, if any, the above-mentioned lady had in his downfall is a matter of dispute. The story rests on Branwell's evidence only, and he is a bad witness. Mrs. Gaskell believed it; but she was not given to suspicion and she had to retract. Did his sisters believe him? There is nothing in Anne's 'unhappy experiences' at Thorpe Green or in Charlotte's allusions to her brother's vices, which necessarily means more than opium and secret drinking; and it seems unlikely that the lady's two daughters would have been allowed to visit Anne at the Parsonage, shortly after Branwell's death, and would have been welcomed there, if there had been a family scandal. In any case, the question is of small importance. Weak people always attribute their failures to somebody else's malign influence, and Branwell was worse than weak. With or without Thorpe Green he would have found his way down hill.

Even when it is stripped of its accretions, the story of the Brontës has all the interest, excitement, and pathos of the best novels, and many people are thrilled by it who never read their books. They want to know more. That more is supplied by the imaginative writer. A legend may be shown to be a legend a dozen times and more; if it supplies a felt want, it survives and becomes immortal, so probably Branwell will always hover at the back of *Wuthering Heights*; Emily will drop a comb into

H

49

the cinders, and rescue her brother from a fiery bed; Mr. Brontë will burn his children's boots, and Charlotte will be the submissive daughter of a tyrannical father. For the general public has a keener appetite for thrills than for facts.

Note. It is only fair to say that in a later and valuable contribution to literature (*Grands Écrivains d'Outre-Manche*, 1901) Madame Duclaux (*née* A. Mary F. Robinson) is herself critical of her earlier work.

4. Dr. Arnold

IT is always easy to make fun of schoolmasters; their daily lives are lived in public before the most critical of audiences, and they have little chance of concealing any of the infirmities which are inherent in human nature. It is still easier to make fun of head masters; they are dressed in the 'little brief authority' which is a challenge to the caricaturist, and, as they frequently have to make important decisions without much time for reflection, they are certain to make mistakes. It is easiest of all, perhaps, to make fun of Dr. Arnold; he was not only a head master, but an intensely earnest one, without the sense of humour which might have saved him from emphasizing the weaker side of those qualities in him which made for greatness; and nothing lends itself so readily to ridicule as moral earnestness.

In *Eminent Victorians* Mr. Lytton Strachey took full advantage of his opportunities for poking grave, ironical fun, and if his gibes are sometimes a little cheap, at their best they are extremely diverting. By treating Dr. Arnold as if he had died yesterday and not in 1842, by detaching him from his surroundings and setting him in the midst of our own social conditions and conventions, Mr. Strachey was able to present him as an incongruous and amusing figure. The admirers of Dr. Arnold have no real quarrel with Mr. Strachey. It is good

for all of us to be laughed at; it helps us not to
get ourselves out of perspective. It would have
been good for Dr. Arnold. Whatever is great in
a man survives ridicule, and he does not cease to
be great because his greatness is interwoven with
foibles. There is nothing to be gained by standing
hat in hand before his foibles.

But, if we really wish to discover why certain
people were regarded as eminent in their own age,
we must not detach them from their surroundings.
However original a man may be, his attitude of
mind is inevitably affected by the beliefs and conventions of his day, and not least by the limitations
in the accumulated store of knowledge and experience which is available for him. The problems
with which he has to deal, though they may be
fundamentally the same as our own, do not present
themselves in precisely the same form and are not
capable of the same solutions. If he is a man of
action, eager to build a New Jerusalem, he will be
compelled to make compromises with the slower
spirits of his age, and however free he may be from
the worst prejudices of his day, he is sure to carry
with him something of the atmosphere which sur-
rounded his childhood. Dr. Arnold was serious in
an age which was accustomed to talk seriously, and
which was not afraid of expressing its religious
convictions. It expressed them on occasions which
we should regard as inappropriate. It was fond of
quoting from the Bible; it was more tolerant of
cant than of levity. It would not have understood

our reluctance to commit ourselves to binding religious dogmas or our habit of understating our deeper emotions and convictions. Dr. Arnold was a deeply religious man, at times perhaps almost morbidly so. Religion coloured the whole of his life, and though his attempts to rationalize his intuitive convictions were not always very happy, he was a dynamic spiritual force of immense power. But there was always a struggle going on in the centre of his soul, a clash of conflicting emotions. His attitude to sin was that of the great Hebrew prophets; he feared it, he hated it, with a peculiar intensity of feeling. But his favourite reading was St. John. In his dealings with boys the voices of the prophets sometimes drowned the voice of the Apostle. Love, if it is to be fruitful, must needs be stern, but in his hatred of their offences the head master was inclined to forget the immaturity of the offenders and the strength of their temptations.

In the seriousness of his outlook and the language in which he expressed it, Dr. Arnold reflected, on the whole, the attitude of the thinking part of his own generation. He would no doubt have thought us flippant; our grandchildren will perhaps think the same. For the tone and temper of any age are peculiar to itself and pass with it. In order to understand what our grandfathers really meant, we have often to translate their words into a more modern style. Thus when Dr. Arnold wrote:

'Rather than have Physical Science the principal thing in my son's mind, I would gladly have him think that the

sun went round the earth and that the stars were mere
spangles set in a bright blue firmament. Surely the one
thing needful for a Christian and an Englishman to study
is Christian, and moral and political philosophy?'

What he really meant was that, if he had to choose
between Natural Science and the Humanities as
the sole basis of education, he would unhesitatingly
choose the Humanities. There are still many
people who will subscribe to that sentiment.

Dr. Arnold's interests were not confined to
education. He had ideas of his own about Church
and State, which excited some interest, as well as
controversy, in his day. But it was as a stimulator
of thought in others, rather than as a propagandist
of new ideas that Dr. Arnold most influenced his
own generation. His was, no doubt, a masterful
personality, and he certainly succeeded in impress-
ing his pupils with his own belief that life was a
serious business—as perhaps it is. But he did not
impose his own views on them unduly. His zeal
was not that of the fanatic, but of one who is a
passionate seeker after truth, and the boys who
grew up under his influence grew up with indepen-
dent minds and judgements. It could never be
said of men so different as Dean Stanley, Tom
Hughes, Clough, Matthew Arnold, and Coning-
ton, that they had been forced into a single mould.
And so it came about that, by the second half of
the 1830's, a number of quite intelligent people,
who did not always see eye to eye with Dr. Arnold
on questions of religion or politics, and who would

not otherwise have sent their sons to a public school at all, were sending them to Rugby, to grow up under the eye of its head master.

What was the secret of Dr. Arnold's success as a head master, at least in his own day? Acting on what principles did he manage to make of Rugby a place to which people, not otherwise favourably disposed to the public schools, were anxious to send their sons?

It must be admitted frankly that those principles were, in the main, not of the kind that is likely to commend itself to the more advanced school of modern educational thought. But one step forward Dr. Arnold did take on what was admittedly the path of progress. He recognized the necessity of broadening the then very narrow basis of education, and he admitted modern history, mathematics, and French into the school curriculum—in small doses, it is true, and not very effectively. Science he rejected, not because he was uninterested in science, but because he thought that, if it was to be studied profitably, it would take up more time than he was prepared to spare from the classics. It is easy to scoff at the meagreness of Dr. Arnold's achievement on these lines, but critics are apt to forget that new subjects cannot be taught at school without new teachers, and that a head master cannot create new teachers with a stroke of the pen. Even at the present day the curricula of the public schools are to some extent controlled by the Universities, and in the 1830's Oxford and

Cambridge were almost sovereign and could 'dispose and bid what shall be right'. With the teaching at his disposal and under the circumstances of the time, it is questionable whether Dr. Arnold could have gone farther than he did. In any case, he lit a candle in England, even though it were a small one, which was destined not to be put out.

But, though his intellectual interests were keen and his mind alert, his main preoccupation as a head master lay in another direction. The educational system which he built up at Rugby was based upon two ideas. In the first place he held that the ultimate value of knowledge to the learner depends on the kind of character on to which it is grafted, and that the mere acquisition of knowledge is not the purpose of life. In other words, he put character first. In the second place he had grasped the unpalatable truth that a boarding-school is not a place for everybody, and that (the words are his own) the first, second, and third duty of a head master is to get rid of unpromising material. This aphorism must sound so harshly in many ears, that a few words of explanation are necessary.

Life at a boarding-school is of necessity in some of its aspects an unnatural life. Boys are removed from the influences of home and more particularly from those of mother and sisters. As they are inevitably segregated into small communities, the traditions of their house and school, the public opinion and moral standards of their companions, exert a heavy and continuous pressure on them, especially in their earlier years. The dangers inherent in the system were even more pronounced in the 1830's than they are to-day, because boys often came to school at a very early age, and, as there were only two terms in the year, and, with fewer facilities for travelling, parents seldom visited their sons at school, the separation from home was longer and more complete. At its best a boarding-house is as happy and wholesome a place for boys as could well be devised; at its worst it is a nightmare, especially for the younger boys. Whether it is a wholesome or an unwholesome place depends on whether its public opinion is formed by the right kind of boy or by the wrong kind of boy. Dr. Arnold did not make the mistake (a not uncommon one) of supposing that boys are so much raw material which, poured into the school machine, will come out of it automatically stamped with the required pattern. For different boys respond very differently to ideals. There are some whom the healthiest school cannot assimilate, any more than the soundest timber can assimilate dry rot. Their continued presence is a danger both to themselves and to others. This, of course, does not mean that such boys are wholly bad. It only means that at a public school they develop their worst qualities, while they help to make the system unworkable and, too often, a sham. Holding these convictions, Dr. Arnold could not but come to the conclusion that one of his principal duties was to eliminate the wrong boys. The difficult problem

I

of what is to be done with the boys who are not fitted for life at a boarding-school was much less acute in the 1830's than it is to-day, because there was no kind of social disqualification in not having been to a public school.

The right boys Dr. Arnold defined as 'Christian gentlemen', a claim which had almost the sting of a paradox at a time when it was hardly expected of schoolboys that they would behave like Christians or like gentlemen, but which now sounds rather pretentious. What, in practice, Dr. Arnold meant by his 'Christian gentlemen' was boys who were capable of responding to Christian ethical ideals, and therefore capable of learning to regard themselves as members of a community in which the personal inclinations of the individual must often be subordinated to the interests of the community as a whole. By whatever name we choose to call it, that spirit, and that only, wherever it prevails, makes of the public schools a national asset.

It is a proof of Dr. Arnold's sanity that he recognized the limits of his personal influence. The potential extent of a head master's influence can hardly be exaggerated. He is the chief source of spiritual and intellectual inspiration. Where he has neither, there may be efficiency, but there will be no vision in the school. But for the average boy in his earlier years the words spoken from the pulpit or in the study count less deeply than the public opinion of his fellows. The more impressionable he seems in his master's study, the more certain he is to be moulded by the tone which prevails on the other side of the swing doors, and from which there is no escape. And that tone depends on the character of the elder boys, and on the kind of discipline which they exercise. Dr. Arnold made the members of his Sixth Form, individually and collectively, responsible for the good tone of the School, and entrusted them with its internal discipline, laying down the general principles on which they were to act, but leaving them a wide discretion in matters of detail. In order to enhance their prestige, and to enable them to perform their duties more effectively, he gave them considerable privileges. But—and it is a very big but—though he did not expect the boys whom he so trusted to be always wise and always effective, any serious and conscious breach of duty entailed grave consequences; for it is impossible to establish a tradition of responsibility among boys or men, unless such failures are dealt with strongly.

In making his Sixth Form automatically a ruling body in the School, Dr. Arnold set a precedent which has not generally been followed by other head masters. The Prefect system which selects those 'by choice or place the worthiest' is not Arnold's system. He definitely meant to make of his Sixth Form a governing class, and believed that they would rise to the occasion. It is not the purpose of this essay to discuss which of the two systems is the better. Both have worked well, and both have failed. Everything depends on the judgement of the head master, his power of inspiring others, and his example. If he does not enforce discipline himself, he can hardly expect his boys to do so.

Dr. Arnold was certainly a stern disciplinarian, but his severity has been not a little exaggerated, and much too much is made of his use of the rod. A birching was in the 1830's, and for some time afterwards, the traditional punishment for school offences, many of which would now be treated far more leniently. But it was not felt to be cruel either by the boys or by their parents. Probably Dr. Arnold, like many other head masters, regarded these whippings as one of the more repugnant of the duties imposed on him by his office, and as the boys recognized in him a man of genuine convictions and not a bully, they did not cease to respect him because he could on occasions be severe. A certain fear of his head master is the beginning (though not the end) of wisdom in a schoolboy, if by fear is meant a certainty that the head master is not afraid of boys, that he cannot be humbugged, and that he will not overlook wrongdoing. Boys are seldom averse from discipline, when it is enforced impartially. They like to know exactly how they stand, what will be tolerated, and what not. It saves them from temptations, and makes life far easier and happier for the smaller boys. What they do dislike is a capricious code of justice which varies with the mood of those who administer it, and which gives preferential treatment to favoured or important individuals. Dr. Arnold was a thoroughly known quantity, and his impartiality was above suspicion. To the new boys he was Black Tom, a figure inspiring awe rather than terror. As they grew and came under his personal influence, the feeling of awe changed to one of profound respect, and often of affection. Perhaps the rising generation will be inclined to wonder whether a man of such a stern exterior and of such unbending principles could have inspired so gentle a feeling as affection in his pupils; but for anybody who in his youth heard old Rugbeians talking of their great head master there is no room for doubt. Dr. Arnold undoubtedly had his limitations, some of them peculiar to his epoch, some inherent in his own character, whose strength lay in the concentration of his purpose rather than in the breadth of his sympathies. But he was capable of winning a devotion which is never given to those who are merely high-principled, and zealous, and stern.

At the fiftieth anniversary of his death there was a rather curious scene at Rugby. Tom Hughes was speaking to the boys in the new Big School on Sunday evening. They had been puzzled, and slightly bored, by the earlier part of the address which, not too tactfully, had been directed against Unitarians and Roman Catholics; but when the speaker started on a personal reminiscence, they.

pricked up their ears. Tom Hughes was about to make a very painful confession, but of this his audience had no suspicion. He told how, on the last night of his last Term, he had given a leaving supper to some of his friends in what was called 'the Fifth Form Room' in the School House—a form of entertainment which had been forbidden by Dr. Arnold. He paused under the influence of strong emotion and then added, a little jerkily, 'The next morning I went home by an early train'. Boys are quick to see the humorous, but not equally quick at probing the deeper feelings, and there was a burst of laughter. Tom Hughes was disconcerted by it for a moment; but he made no comment, and went on to read in a voice, of unmistakably deep emotion, the letter which he had received a few days afterwards, from Dr. Arnold, a kind letter, but one of straightforward rebuke and disappointment. Then he added, amidst a profound silence, 'And the next thing I heard was that he was dead'. It is possible that to some this incident may sound only like an echo of Victorian sentimentality; yet to those who witnessed it the bitterness of the regret which, after so many years, impelled Tom Hughes to do public penance, as it were, for a thoughtless act of disloyalty to his head master, was full of significance.

And there is the testimony of Matthew Arnold in *Rugby Chapel*, one of the most original of his poems. A son may be suspected of partiality, but the tribute which Matthew Arnold paid to his

father was not held by his contemporaries to be
exaggerated.

> But thou would'st not *alone*
> Be saved, my father! *alone*
> Conquer and come to thy goal,
> Leaving the rest in the wild.
>
> .   .   .   .   .   .
>
> And through thee I believe
> In the noble and great who are gone;
> Pure souls honour'd and blest
> By former ages, who else
>
> .   .   .   .   .   .
>
> Seem'd but a dream of the heart,
> Seem'd but a cry of desire.
> Yes! I believe that there lived
> Others like thee in the past,
>
> .   .   .   .   .   .
>
> ... souls temper'd with fire,
> Fervent, heroic, and good,
> Helpers and friends of mankind.
>
> .   .   .   .   .   .
>
> Beacons of hope, ye appear!
> Languor is not in your heart,
> Weakness is not in your word,
> Weariness not on your brow.
>
> .   .   .   .   .   .
>
> Ye move through the ranks, recall
> The stragglers, refresh the outworn,
> Praise, re-inspire the brave!
> Order, courage, return.
> Eyes rekindling, and prayers,
> Follow your steps as ye go.
> Ye fill up the gaps in our files,

Strengthen the wavering line,
Stablish, continue our march,
On, to the bound of the waste,
On, to the City of God.

That, of course, was not how Mr. Lytton Strachey saw Dr. Arnold, when he conjured up his eminent Victorians, and with an ironic smile stripped them of their robes. But Mr. Strachey, too, had his limitations, and in his keen appreciation of the littleness of life he sometimes failed to see its greatness.

5. The Country Parson

WHEN the Rev. James Woodforde, Rector of Weston in the County of Norfolk, died, so to speak, for the second time, in 1931 with the publication of the fifth, and last, volume of his private diary, he had become intimately known to a much wider world than was the case when his parishioners followed him to the grave in the January of 1803. Whether he would have enjoyed the prospect of such a posthumous fame is highly doubtful; more probably, if he could have foreseen it, he would have taken the necessary steps to render it impossible. For he was by nature a secretive man who resented any intrusion upon his private affairs, and though he was probably quite unconscious that in his later years his diary had become largely a revelation of his own failings, he must have been aware that, scattered throughout its pages, there were passages that would inevitably excite a curiosity about himself, which he would have been the last person to encourage. Fortunately for us, he could not 'look into the seeds of time', and his executors piously spared a personal record which probably they never attempted to read.

It is a strange and a tantalizing record, one of the strangest and most tantalizing ever compiled. To some readers, indeed, and particularly to those who read hastily, it is simply a tedious brief chronicle of the smallest of small beer. Parson

Woodforde was certainly no Pepys. He had neither the insatiable curiosity nor the infinite zest in life of that prince of diarists. Nor had he any itch to put the whole of himself on to paper. On the contrary, he practised an often exasperating caution, and kept a careful watch on his pen, lest by any chance it should furnish matter which might conceivably be used against him. Thus, for example, when the Income-tax had become law, and our Parson had assessed his own income at what was patently an optimistically low figure, he ceased to enter in his diary his annual receipts for tithe, hitherto one of the most interesting items of his December audit 'frolic'. He will sometimes hint at family or other private scandals, but the hint never matures into a revelation. Often, too, he will express his displeasure with individuals, but he seldom vouchsafes the real cause of his anger. All that he actually meant to do was to keep a concise and accurate record of the weather, of current expenses and receipts, of where he 'breakfasted, dined, supped and slept', of how he occupied his day, of his own health and that of the inmates of his household, of the duties he performed (or failed to perform) at church, and, last but not least, of what he ate for dinner.

But the cumulative effect of these trivial entries is surprising. At the end of them we know exactly what it was like to live in a country parsonage in Norfolk in the last quarter of the eighteenth century. For more than thirty years we rise every morning with the diarist and follow him through his daily round of simple pleasures and even simpler duties. We see him at work in his garden or coursing a hare with his greyhounds, or dragging his pond for fish, or brewing beer and bottling wine. We help him on to his horse, or later into his 'little new cart', to pay a morning call on some neighbour clergyman and earn an appetite for dinner. We watch the harvest ripening on his glebe, and rejoice with him when Ben Leggatt, his farming man, returns from Norwich sober and with a good price for the corn, barley, or oats, which he has carried to Mr. Bloome in the 'great cart'. Again we rejoice when the tithe audit 'frolic' is safely over and nobody has been offensively drunk. We feel with him the bitter cold of those Norfolk winters when 'the chambers froze above stairs', and the study fire could not coax the thermometer above the region of the 40° Fahrenheit, and we sit up with him in the same study when the night winds are howling, and he dares not go to bed. For was he not brought up on tales of the great storm which swept over England in 1705, and sent a chimney crashing through the roof of the palace at Wells to kill the Bishop in his bedroom? And is there not just such another chimney on the roof of Weston Parsonage? We entertain, and are entertained by, his friends at Gargantuan feasts, the mere thought of which makes the imagination green and pale. But our Parson and his generation were heroic eaters. He had a high regard for God's great gift of food, and loved to see it reverently treated. Even if he has been too bilious to partake himself, he rolls out the long list of noble dishes for us in his diary, like a hymn of praise; and if there has been any breach in the sacred ritual or a great dish has been dishonoured, if the mackerel was unaccompanied by gooseberry sauce, or the haunch of venison ill cooked and badly served, he lets us know it.

As a result of these same Gargantuan feasts, we stand with him bare-footed on the cold hearth-stone when cramp has seized him by the leg, or ache with him in a sleepless bed when gout is 'playing the devil with his great toe'. Fain would we persuade him, if we might, that eight glasses of port wine after dinner are not the best remedy for his complaint, but we should get little support from Dr. Thorne of Mattishall, his medical adviser. At not infrequent intervals we accompany him on a jaunt to Norwich, to pay bills, do some shopping, dine with Mr. Priest his wine merchant, and see a play. And every now and again, when summer is at its height, we pack our trunks and take our places in the London coach on the first stage of the long journey to Somerset, the home-land of the Wood-fordes, there to stay with hospitable sister Pounsett, and feast on salmon and duck, on pork and peas, and to walk, and fish, and renew old friendships and revive old memories, till the approach of winter sends us home again to Weston, rejuvenated by the genial climate of the West Country, but 'a little low at parting from our friends'.

Meanwhile, by slow degrees, we are making the acquaintance of people whom we should be sorry not to have known: of the Bodhams of Mattishall, more cultured than most of their neighbours, of merry old Mr. Du Quesne, the bachelor Rector of East Tuddenham, who once made fun of the Parson's gout and was never quite forgiven for it, and, best of all, of Mr. Custance (our squire at Weston House), and his wife, that charming pair of perfect English gentlefolk, so unostentatious in their use of wealth, so generous in their thoughts and actions, so considerate to all alike, rich and poor, equals and dependants, that nothing is recorded of them which is not to their praise. Their mansion has shared the fate of many another stately country house in these lean years. It has been demolished, and their portraits no longer look down from its walls upon a place which has become strangely familiar to us; but their memory still lives green in the pages of our Country Parson's diary.

All this is much; but it does not exhaust the human interest of this amazing journal. James Woodforde was reticence personified, but when a man is reviewing in his mind the happenings of the day and has a pen in his hand, pride, or pique, or anger, or fear, will sometimes prove stronger than discretion, and down will go some revealing words which throw a light on what had previously been obscure or lend a significance to what seemed trivial and irrelevant. With his diary before us and a little reading between its lines we know Parson

Woodforde better probably than he ever knew himself. We can picture him, not only as he appeared to himself, but also (a very different matter) as he must have appeared to the little world in which he moved. Looking at him thus from the outside, we see in him a man timidly selfish, but often moved by kindly impulses; rather tepid in his affections, and more capable of friendliness than of friendship; courteous, and a generous giver, but critical of others and niggardly of praise, one, moreover, who under a placid exterior could harbour long resentments; proud of his good breeding, but not always remarkable for his good taste, and something of a snob; much occupied with his private concerns, but intellectually idle; a good master, but a bad minister, and an adept at the gentle art of self-deception. We note how deftly, by the use of a single epithet, 'my *honest* smuggler', he brings a dubious practice within the bounds of the moral law: how easily he persuades a not exacting conscience that his pleasant vices are not vices at all, but the wisdom of Solomon. We note too how very lightly his cure of souls sits on his conscience, though in this respect he does not seem to have differed materially from the other clergy in the diocese. One service, and one only, on Sundays, sometimes in the morning and sometimes in the afternoon: a special service on Christmas Day, Ash Wednesday, and Good Friday: three celebrations of the Holy Communion, on Christmas Day, Easter Sunday, and Whit-Sunday respectively—

that was all that 'duty' demanded of him, and all that he ever gave in his most active years. For the rest, he baptized, married, churched, and buried his parishioners for the customary fee, which he always returned to the poor and needy, for Parson Woodforde was never mean or grasping over money. He was philanthropic according to his lights; no disabled soldier, genuine or spurious, ever begged of him in vain. But it must be admitted that, even in his most generous years, his charities (and he recorded them down to the pence) make but a poor showing in comparison with his wine bills. He was friendly, but not too familiar, with his farmers. Of the poor he was somewhat afraid, especially in times of dearth, but he was genuinely sorry for their sufferings and generous with shillings and sixpences. He visited the sick and the dying, when they sent for him, cheered their last hours with some favourite viand of his or theirs from his kitchen, and, when they were dead, believed that they had gone to a happier existence. On the whole, his parishioners seem to have liked him, for he was a kindly man and his besetting sins were mostly of a kind that harmed nobody but himself. After all, if one were *in extremis*, it would be more comforting to be wafted to Heaven on a breast of veal from Parson Woodforde, than to eternal fire on an Evangelical tract.

But his heart was never really in his vocation, except in so far as that vocation included the proper cultivation of his glebe land. Any emotional fervour in 'serving the Lord' we could hardly expect from him; in a Fellow of New College at that period it would have been bad form and smacking of dissent. But, in truth, he does not seem to have been, in any real sense of the word, a religious man at all. His diary, it is true, contains many conventional expressions of thanks to Almighty God for a good harvest, a good appetite, improved health or safe return from a journey, but there is no mention of family prayers. We do not know whether he preached his own sermons, but we venture to doubt it. At all events, there is no record of his having written one at Weston and, when he was invited to preach in Norwich Cathedral on a special occasion, far from being gratified he was seriously annoyed. For the rites of the church, which he was ordained to perform, he can have had very little feeling. After the Easter Sunday of 1797, although he was up and about and able to brew beer, he ceased to attend divine worship and, stranger still, never again received the Holy Sacrament—unless it was administered to him on his death-bed. Long before this, however, we had observed in him a growing distaste for being in church, whether as officiating priest or as one of the congregation—a distaste which gradually grew into a pronounced phobia.

The crisis came one cold Christmas morning (in 1794) when the Parson, who had just finished reading the morning service, had a fit in his desk. He calls it an epileptic seizure, but it was certainly not that. It was of short duration, and he was able to administer the Holy Sacrament and walk home. But his nerve was badly shaken, and from that time forward the fear of another break-down became an obsession with him. For a while he struggled feebly to overcome it, but on many a Sunday there was no service at Weston Church; either the weather was too inclement or the Parson was too unwell. Finally he threw up the sponge and entrusted his clerical duties to a succession of curates who combined them with others of a similar nature elsewhere, and generally performed them, somewhat perfunctorily, at a yearly stipend of £30. From that time onwards, so far as the needs of his parish were concerned, the Rector of Weston might just as well have been living in the antipodes.

But with all his shortcomings, and although he fails at any period of his career to win our whole-hearted esteem, James Woodforde never wholly alienates our sympathies. There was a funda-mental simplicity in the man, even in his self-deceptions, which is engaging, and we never cease to share his interest in a life so full and yet so empty and unimaginative, that the loss of the American Colonies, the French Revolution, and the Napo-leonic wars, hardly stirred a ripple on its placid surface.

But we are sorry for Nancy, his niece and com-panion, who experienced all the emptiness of that life and none of its fullness. It is true that we are never conscious of any personal charm about her, and probably if we had met her in the flesh, we should not have taken to her; she was too much like her brother William. But we are sorry for her. She had come into Norfolk as a girl, and as the uneventful days passed by, her youth passed with them; its desires unsatisfied, its hopes unfulfilled. No wonder if she was sometimes bored and restless. The frequent recurrence of this disgruntled mood perplexed and distressed her worthy uncle. What ailed the silly girl? Had she not the society of the Custances, of good old Mr. and Mrs. Bodham, and of good old Mr. Du Quesne? Did she not live on the best of meat and drink? Did he not take her sometimes to Norwich to do her shopping and see a play or hear the *Messiah*? Did he not play cribbage with her of an evening—a game at which he always won? Did he not give her a yearly allowance of £10, and throw in a pig, reared, fattened, killed, and sold at his own expense and for her exclusive benefit? What more could a girl want?

But Nancy wanted more. She wanted companions of her own age, she wanted fun, she wanted adventure; probably she wanted a husband. Life beckoned from afar, but it never came to Weston Parsonage to break its dull, monotonous routine. Once she took the bit between her teeth (for the Woodfordes were a self-willed race) and went in search of life, in the company of Betsy Davey and Mr. Walker, and in a manner which might well have proved socially disastrous. But of that more anon. So the irrevocable years went by, and a prolonged illness, which ultimately cured itself, in spite of Dr. Thorne's vomits and purges and her uncle's port, took the bloom off her youth, and gradually she ceased to be counted among the 'young people' and became an old maid.

One thing Mr. Woodforde might have done and failed to do: he might have saved money on his drink bills, and his food bills, and his other bills, and made sure that his niece should enjoy a dignified independence when he himself went the way of all Rectors of Weston and slept in the chancel. But, as the probate of his will discloses, he never saved a penny, and though he made her one of his two residuary legatees, when debts, and funeral and other expenses had been paid, there could not have been more than about £200 in cash and the small property in Somerset, to be divided between Nancy and her brother William.

We have said that in this diary there is much to be read between the lines, and some of it is legible enough. But there is one secret so jealously guarded, that it defies all attempts to penetrate it. We will call it 'the *affaire* Davey'. At the time of our story Mrs. Davey was living in rooms at Mattishall, and if the Parson had written sonnets like Shakespeare, she would certainly have figured in them as the counterpart of the 'dark lady', for she seems alternately to have attracted him by her person and repelled him by her affectations. He made her acquaintance on his first visit to his future living, when she threw herself at the head of his

companion, and she flits through all the early and
middle years of his life at Weston, an arch, vulgar,
mischievous widow with an only daughter, setting
her cap now at one, now at another, breeding
jealousies and broils, and thoroughly enjoying
herself. At one time she seems never to be out of
the Parsonage. What was her game? Did she
seriously try to hook Mr. Woodforde or was she
only flirting with him? And he; was he really
enamoured of her and jealous of rivals, or did he
only tolerate the mother for the sake of the daughter? We know that he was sentimentally attracted
by pretty and vivacious flappers, and 'my dear
Betsy Davey' was both. She was, moreover, the
only friend of her own age whom Nancy possessed
in East Anglia. We should like to think that our
Parson was thinking chiefly of his niece; but we
cannot forget that really unseemly romp in the
parlour (or was it the study?) when he captured one
of the widow's garters, and was so proud of the
exploit that he could not refrain from boasting of
it in his diary. And what, we wonder, were other
people thinking and saying? Did the dear man
suppose that, because diaries are dumb, walls have
no ears and servants no curiosity? We cannot
answer any of these questions, but we are relieved
when the storm centre shifts from Weston to
Mattishall and gathers round the head of Mr.
Smith, a brother clergyman (not to be confused
with another of the same name and place, who
appears later in the diary). We have made the

acquaintance of Mr. Smith at 'rotation' dinners and elsewhere, have welcomed him as a new friend, and supposed him, perhaps without any sufficient reason, to be a man of solid worth and sober judgement. We are surprised therefore when we learn that he and Mrs. Davey are about to be married. But on the eve of wedding bells there is a rupture. Somehow or other, though we do not know how, Parson Woodforde must have been more personally interested in the matter than the diary admits, for Mr. Smith insisted on seeing him personally and making his own position perfectly clear. And relations between the two men must have become seriously strained, for the meeting took place, not at the Parsonage, but on severely neutral ground, namely, in Weston Churchyard. What passed at that interview the diary, to our grievous disappointment, does not relate; it only observes that, if what Mr. Smith said was true, he (Mr. Smith) had been very badly treated.

Now we feel sure that what Mr. Smith said was true, and we confidently expect to see no more of Mrs. Davey. But a fresh surprise is in store for us. Mrs. Davey reappears at the Parsonage, no longer cordially welcomed, but still received. It is Mr. Smith who disappears from the diary. No more 'rotation' dinners, and hosts and hostesses have to be careful not to include Mr. Woodforde and Mr. Smith on the same invitation list. Years afterwards the two men met on the road between Weston and Norwich, and passed each other in embarrassed silence. More years, and Mr. Smith held out an olive branch. He sent his servant lad with kind inquiries, when the Woodfordes returned from Somerset in the autumn of 1795. Mr. Woodforde thought it 'strange' and made no gesture in reply—an unforgiving man, though we shall never know what exactly it was that he could not or would not forgive.

Incidentally, 'the *affaire* Davey' led to a temporary breach with Dr. Thorne, a connexion of the lady's, and somehow involved in the embroglio. But in this instance Mr. Woodforde was obliged to practise forgiveness, for, after trying in vain to cure a gouty sore on his leg by quack remedies and the light of nature, he had to swallow his pride and send for the doctor, and, as the wound yielded to treatment, friendly relations were restored.

But to return to the Daveys. After the rupture with Mr. Smith the widow left Mattishall for a season; but no sooner was the mother off the scene than the daughter took up the running. She had become engaged to a Mr. Walker, a dissolute young man with neither private means nor prospects, though he affected to possess both. The young couple quartered themselves more or less permanently at the Parsonage, and, aided and abetted by Nancy, could not be dislodged. Mr. Walker would take a long farewell after breakfast, and return unexpectedly to supper. He ceased to be even outwardly civil to his host, and Mr. Woodforde was no longer master in his own house. The young people whispered and giggled in corners, flouted his authority, and made plans behind his back; and one fine day they all drove off together to Norwich and slept a night there, unchaperoned, at the same inn.

Now, when young ladies openly defy the social conventions of their day, they are asking for trouble. We do not know how long it took for the news of this escapade to reach Mattishall and Wytchingham and other interested places within the Woodforde circle, to set tongues wagging. But it must certainly have got there, and we can almost hear kind Mrs. Bodham hoping that the story had been exaggerated, and less kind Mrs. Jeans exclaiming, 'What next?' But there were to be no more escapades. A warrant was out for Mr. Walker's arrest, and, crippled with debts and disease, he went into hiding. He only emerged from it in a hearse, to be buried rather grimly in Weston Churchyard by Parson Woodforde: the one occasion on which that gentleman did not dare, or care, to express a hope that the departed had gone to eternal bliss.

The Daveys both found husbands elsewhere, and vanish from the story—except that Betsy reappears for a few unrevealing moments in the last chapter. But between them they had left the prestige of the Woodfordes badly shaken. Nancy particularly was under a cloud; the diary admits as much, and indeed it could not have been otherwise. It was Mrs. Custance who restored her to a place in the sun. This, to be sure, is only an inference, but it is at least a reasonable one. The bare facts, as revealed in the diary, are as follows. Mr. Townshend (afterwards Lord Bayning) was the biggest wig of the neighbourhood, a bigger wig even than Mr. Custance, and he had asked Messrs. Priest of Reepham, Du Quesne, Jeans, and Woodforde to dinner at Honingham Hall. Neither Mrs. Priest nor Mrs. Jeans nor Miss Woodforde was included in the invitation. But on the Sunday before the party Mr. and Mrs. Townshend, returning from a visit to Weston House, called at the Parsonage 'in their full-bodied coach' with an invitation to Nancy to accompany her uncle. As things turned out, she never actually went to the party. She was to have driven to it in the little open 'cart', and, the weather proving unfavourable, she was obliged to send her excuses instead. But the invitation had been a great whitewashing, and Mr. Woodforde's gratification pierces through his guarded phrases. What Honingham Hall had cleansed nobody could call common or unclean. Now it is extremely improbable that Honingham Hall would have thus suddenly changed its mind, and shown Miss Woodforde this signal mark of its favour (for she was the only lady invited), unless somebody had been pulling wires on her behalf. But, apart from Mr. Du Quesne who, as an old bachelor, would hardly have risked burning his fingers in such a delicate matter, the only friend of Nancy's who had any influence at Honingham Hall was

Mrs. Custance, and Mrs. Custance had had an opportunity of exerting that influence while the Townshends were at Weston House. The deduction therefore seems fairly safe.

Be this as it may, the Woodfordes had no truer friends than the Custances, and it was a black day indeed when the family coach carried that delightful family away to years of exile at Bath and the shutters went up at Weston House; for, with Mr. Du Quesne ageing rapidly and Mr. Bodham sick unto death, the social amenities of life at Weston seemed almost to have reached the vanishing point.

But just when the prospect appeared most gloomy, Fate relented a little. Mr. Stoughton came to Sparham, and with Mr. Mellish and Mr. Corbould youth stepped once more on to the scene. Mr. Mellish had succeeded Mr. Du Quesne at Tuddenham; Mr. Corbould had succeeded nobody, but he had recently taken holy orders and a wife, and had come to live at Hungate Lodge (a short walk from the Parsonage) to fish, to shoot, and to take such duties as the sick, the absent, or the idle among his clerical neighbours might from time to time care to hand over to him. All three clergymen were given to hospitality and possessed of private means. The great days of dinner parties began again, and the standard of entertaining was pushed high, so high that Mr. Woodforde, though recurrent attacks of gout inclined him to be peevish, could find much to praise and little to criticize.

The Parsonage and Hungate Lodge were soon on intimate terms, and we seem to be enjoying an Indian summer in an atmosphere of mutual goodwill and hospitality, when a resounding quarrel 'disturbed the mirth and broke the good company'.

Relations between Weston Parsonage and Wytchingham, though outwardly correct, had never been cordial. There was something about the Jeanses, husband and wife, which jarred on Mr. Woodforde. They expected him to come to dinner at their bidding—often at short notice and to fill a gap—exactly as if they were the Townshends and Wytchingham were Honingham Hall: and they frequently declined his counter-invitations to dine at Weston. Mrs. Jeans was 'consequential' and affected. The Parson constantly reminds his diary how badly Mrs. Jeans manages her household and her dinner parties: how unlike a really great lady. In short, the Jeanses supposed themselves to have come out of a higher and a better drawer than the Woodfordes: an intolerable assumption, and particularly galling after the Daveys had let us down so badly. But the two clergymen were near neighbours, and often had need of one another's services; so although relations were often strained and the interchange of amenities a trifle feline, there had never been any open quarrel. Nor were we expecting one, for when Mr. Woodforde started on what proved to be his last visit to the West Country, the two families seemed to be on unusually good terms. They had been dining at one another's houses and meeting at the houses of mutual friends. The diary gives no hint of any gathering clouds. At Bath Mr. Woodforde called on Mrs. Jeans's aunt, and, though he only stayed a short time, we note the visit as a friendly act. When he returned to Weston early in the November of 1795 his friends and neighbours paid the customary call at the Parsonage, and we notice that Mr. Jeans is not among the number, and we do not meet him at dinner parties. But we assume that he is away from home. He was often away and for long periods. Then one day we observe that, when our Parson goes to Reepham, he reaches it by a new and circuitous route. It is characteristic of him that he mentions the fact, but not the cause. But we know at once what has happened. He is avoiding Wytchingham and the Jeanses.

What was the cause of the quarrel? We shall never know; but we cannot help suspecting that that aunt had something to do with it. Perhaps she repeated to Mr. Woodforde something which the Jeanses had said about him; or perhaps she repeated to the Jeanses something which he told her about them. In any case there was a row royal, and we sense the general *gène*. In a small social circle it is a great misfortune when two of the leading figures fall out. Dinner parties have to be duplicated when the Rector of Weston and the Rector of Wytchingham cannot meet at the same table, and everybody has to be careful what he, or she, says, lest it should be repeated and make more mischief. Probably if the Custances had been at home, they would have poured oil on the troubled waters, and the breach would not have been final; for they were born peace-makers, and Mr. Woodforde was more amenable to their authority than to that of any other living person. But the Custances were still at Bath, and, in their absence, there was nobody to take the lead.

At last Mr. Corbould, greatly daring and prompted, we may suppose, from Wytchingham, tried his hand at peace-making. The Jeanses were contemplating a long removal to London, and the moment seemed propitious for effecting a reconciliation. The first move was in the nature of a *ballon d'essai*. The little Jeanses had been spending the afternoon at Hungate Lodge. On their way home with their nurses they called, without any previous warning, at the Parsonage. They were received with cold civility. Whatever other people might think about them, Mr. Woodforde had never found the little Jeanses irresistible, and no answering dove went out from Weston.

Nothing daunted, Mr. Corbould bided his time and tried again. Somehow or other he persuaded his Rector (for he was now Mr. Woodforde's curate) to meet Mrs. Jeans at dinner at Hungate Lodge. Things looked hopeful for a moment, for Mr. Woodforde (presumably at the dinner) offered to escort Mrs. Jeans over the grounds at Weston House, and to take her afterwards to dinner at the

Parsonage. But everything went wrong. The lady came late to the tryst and kept the Parson waiting, and, if the subsequent entertainment was at all like the record of it in the diary, it must have been as cool as ice. Some weeks afterwards the two hostile Rectors were together, with others, at the house of a mutual friend, but they did not speak to one another. The Jeanses, says the diary, had behaved 'very so so', and they left for London without a blessing.

Mr. Corbould had acted with the best intentions; but his Rector was not a man who liked to have his conduct questioned, even indirectly, and he resented any attempt from outside to intervene in his private concerns. We are not surprised therefore to find that after the failure of the peace negotiations his diary becomes much more critical of Mr. Corbould than it was before, and records some trivial incidents which do not redound to that gentleman's glory. Under the circumstances, we do not take these very seriously. As for Mr. Jeans, like Betsy Davey, he appears again on the stage for a few moments in the last act. His curate in charge had gone to prison for a spirited attempt to fight a duel with an officer, and Mr. Jeans had come back to do duty at Wytchingham till a successor could be found. On his return journey to London he stopped to pay a call at Weston Parsonage. The diary notes that he appeared to be in good health, and that he refused to take any refreshment. We venture to doubt whether the invitation to do so was pressed with any great warmth.

At 55 Parson Woodforde was prematurely old, and the last phase of his life is full of shadows. We had long realized that he was eating and drinking —especially drinking—much more than was good for him, and that, if he did not change his ways, he would never make old bones. When he admitted that at one of his audit 'frolics' he was 'merry, but not so as to be disguised', we wondered whether his parishioners drew the same nice distinction. When, during his last visit to Somerset, he bought three gallons of gin for his private use, and then found fault with his dinner, we conjectured that Sister Pounsett had been trying to ration his consumption of spirits and had probably given him some good advice about his personal habits, and we thought that the subsequent coolness of his attitude towards his once favourite sister might be explained by his unwillingness to receive advice on this subject. Moreover, we had always supposed that Nancy's 'pertness' must sometimes have taken the form of a direct allusion to these same habits, and we wished more power to her elbow. The last years of the diary seem to confirm our worst apprehensions. It is an ominous sign when he takes to procuring his liquor from different sources, as if he did not wish any one purveyor to know how large a quantity was being consumed at the Parsonage. All those gallons of rum, all that vast array of bottles returned empty, tell the same story; for there was nobody now to empty them but the Parson himself; no more guests, no more dinner parties, and Nancy's habitual drink was table beer. We fear that in those closing years, when he was helped up the steep stairs to his bedroom at night, our Parson was not always strictly sober.

But we are somewhat anticipating events. In the May of 1797 Mr. Woodforde had a severe illness, was indeed unconscious for a time and thought to be dying. It would have been happier for him if he had passed away, when Dr. Lubbock was being hastily summoned from Norwich, and Brother John and Nephew William were posting up from Somerset to the sick bed. However, he survived the attack to live for another five and a half years, and it looked at one time as if he might recover that particular combination of minor ailments which for many men after 50 constitutes normal health. But he never gave himself a chance, and his obstinate attempt to win back to strength on a diet of pork, port, and rum, failed as it was bound to fail. Short rallies were followed by long relapses, and with every year he grew increasingly nervous, irritable, and suspicious, depressed in company but afraid to be left alone, full of self-pity, and demanding from others a sympathy which he did not always receive and, we fear, did not always deserve. To the last he clung to his appetite, and thanked God whenever he had been able to eat hearty and with relish.

He must have been a trying man to live with in his last years, and especially for Nancy whom, though he 'crabbed' her in his diary, he would never allow to be long out of the house. Fortunately for her the Custances had returned from Bath and were consistently kind. Singly or in twos and threes they were constantly in and out of the Parsonage; they had her to dinner; they took her for 'airings' in the family coach, and to Norwich to do her shopping; and, when the end came, they carried her off to Weston House till her plans for the future were settled and she went to London to live with her brother Samuel, the R.A.

Dropsy gave the *coup de grâce* to a life which had become a burden to its possessor, and the poor man died on 1 January 1803 and was buried in the chancel of his church. The last years of a man's life are apt to overshadow what has gone before and to make us see the whole in a false perspective. They are not necessarily, and perhaps not often, the real harvest time of life. Mr. Woodforde did not grow old with grace or dignity; but nobody can be sure of emerging with credit from that ordeal, for age is a tricky business, and senility must not be judged by ordinary standards. So we will try to forget that last depressing volume of his diary, and think of 'the Country Parson' as we knew him in his prime, firing off his blunderbuss in honour of the Queen's birthday, or distributing pennies on St. Valentine's day to the village children, or sailing his model frigate on 'the great pond' for the benefit of the little Custances, or fishing the summer streams of his native Somerset. For he was an angler—not with passion nor always according to the strict rules of the art, but still an angler; and by the grace of God and of gentle Isaak Walton all anglers go at last to Heaven.

6. Tennyson's 'In Memoriam'

IF a sexagenarian could revisit the home of his childhood and find it exactly as it was when he left it in his teens, he would probably feel a certain disillusionment. The boundaries of the garden would have contracted, the spacious entrance-hall would have shrunk to the dimensions of a passage, the dining-room and the front staircase would have lost their noble proportions. Nor would all the familiar objects of the interior cast their old spell upon him. That picture, which once seemed the embodiment of a high romance, would offend his taste as morbidly sentimental, the coloured glass of the window on the landing would have lost its glamour, and those vases on the mantelpiece in the drawing-room, which were once the last word in a consummate art, would appear pretentious and even vulgar. Yet in spite of the general shrinkage and a consciousness of the change which time has wrought in his aesthetic values, he might still find in the place and its surroundings a spaciousness, a dignity, and a homely charm, which are lacking in the most up-to-date dwelling of the most perfectly planned garden city.

Somewhat similar sensations are experienced by one, born in the 1860's, who after many years returns to a study of *In Memoriam*, a poem which he discovered for himself in boyhood, devoured with a reverent and uncritical enthusiasm, and believed to be one of the profoundest utterances of the human spirit. It is no longer that. It is not so big as it was, it is not so convincing. A maturer taste recoils from the polish which is too often lavished on the trivial, its mannerisms have lost their charm, some of it is even astonishingly bad. On the other hand, much of it still remains astonishingly good, and the excellence of what is excellent in it—a quiet depth of feeling and simplicity of expression—is heightened for the sexagenarian reader by the reflection (one which never occurred to him in boyhood) that the achievement of *In Memoriam* is an achievement of youth and not of maturer years. For when Arthur Henry Hallam, 'the only begetter' of the poem, died in Vienna in 1833 at the age of 22, Tennyson himself was only 24; and although the poem in its entirety was not published (anonymously) till 1850, almost all the immortal part of it was composed between the years 1833 and 1838. In other words, the solid kernel of great and moving poetry, which is embedded in *In Memoriam*, was the work of Tennyson in his twenties, not of Tennyson the accepted 'Bard' of the middle-Victorian epoch. If we bear this fact in mind, we are the better able to discount and to pardon blemishes which we expect to find in the work of young poets, and amongst them a certain lack of perspective. For example, the pathos of Hallam's early death would not be less, if his merits and his promise were presented to us in less superlative terms. We have learnt by experience that 'the rapt oration flowing free' in College rooms 'from point to point with power and grace' does not necessarily herald 'a pillar of the state' and lead to Downing Street or the Woolsack; and we cannot help being impressed by the fact that Hallam competed three times unsuccessfully for the Chancellor's medal, and failed to take his degree. But youth takes itself and its friends very seriously, and the inspired utterances of an undergraduate of 19 on such topics as 'Mind and Art, and Labour, and the changing mart, and all the frame-work of the land' are eagerly accepted as 'heavenly-wise' by his admiring contemporaries. It is probable therefore that 'the Apostles', as that 'band of youthful friends' was dubbed at Cambridge, somewhat over-rated Hallam's abilities; what is beyond question is that by his premature death the world was robbed of a very attractive personality.

Again, I think that most readers of *In Memoriam* would feel more comfortable if Tennyson had expressed his personal reaction to his young friend's charm in language less definitely connubial. He could, of course, plead the example of Shakespeare, and it is obvious that the *Sonnets* were constantly in his mind. But if such language is to be used at all, it must be used robustly, and Tennyson was not robust. Such lines as (LX)

> My spirit loved and loves him yet,
> Like some poor girl whose heart is set
> On one whose rank exceeds her own,

are mawkish rather than moving. In literature a certain reticence in the language both of grief and of affection is more telling than a complete unpacking of the heart in words. It is better to say too little than to say too much. 'Dear' is preferable to 'dearest'; nor do I think that 'My Arthur' is a happy alternative to 'My comrade', if only for the reason that the poetic value of Christian names, especially men's Christian names, is liable to violent fluctuations. But Tennyson was a young man, and the friendship with Hallam had been for him a unique experience. To the home-bred poet of 19 who had been unable to endure the rough-and-tumble of school life, shy and morbidly sensitive to ridicule, ambitious but shrinking from contacts with the herd, this fine flower of Eton culture with his personal charm, his social graces, his lively brain, and enthusiastic interests, had indeed appeared as 'half-divine'.

And worship on the one side was repaid with homage on the other. It was Hallam who discovered Tennyson at Cambridge, thawed his reserve and drew him from his gloomy isolation, if not into the limelight, at least into the luminous circle of 'the Apostles', where he would sit apart and enjoy the oratorical triumphs of his friend. The joy of such a mutual friendship, a 'marriage of true minds', is felicitously described in *In Memoriam* in XXIII, for example:

> When each by turns was guide to each,
> And Fancy light from Fancy caught,

93

> And Thought leapt out to wed with Thoug
> Ere Thought could wed itself with Speech;

and with greater depth of feeling in xxv,

> I know that this was Life,—the track
> Whereon with equal feet we fared;
> And then, as now, the day prepared
> The daily burden for the back.
>
> But this it was that made me move
> As light as carrier-birds in air;
> I loved the weight I had to bear,
> Because it needed help of Love:

and again in LXXIX (addressed to his brother)

> And so my wealth resembles thine,
> But he was rich where I was poor,
> And he supplied my want the more
> As his unlikeness fitted mine.

The loss of his first and only really intimate friend would have been a heavy blow to Tennyson at any time, but the loss occurred at a moment when that friend could least be spared. As has been already said, Tennyson was both ambitious and timid. He dreaded criticism, and above all he dreaded ridicule. Hallam had done much to foster his ambition and fortify his self-confidence, and at the end of 1832 Tennyson had published his second[1] volume of verse. It included such poems as *The Lady of Shallot*, *The Lotos-Eaters*, and the first version of *Oenone*, but the reviewers, and especially Lockhart, fell upon it with a sustained

[1] Not counting the early 'Poems by two Brothers'.

94

scorn which was more eloquent of bad temper than of sound judgement. Most of the ridicule was puerile, much of the criticism doctrinaire and undiscerning, but before the violence of this concentrated and unexpected storm Tennyson wilted and very nearly collapsed. The one man capable of rekindling his courage and helping him to see things in their true perspective was snatched away by death. Thus the bewildering sense of bereavement synchronized with a bewildering sense of failure, and for ten years the young poet relapsed into a moody and miserable silence.

What is enduring in *In Memoriam* is the reflection of his mind under this double shock during the early half of those ten years, and more particularly during the early months when he was writing not for publication but as an outlet for his own sorrow. (v).

> I sometimes hold it half a sin
>   To put in words the grief I feel;
>   For words, like Nature, half reveal
> And half conceal the Soul within.

> But, for the unquiet heart and brain,
>   A use in measured language lies;
>   The sad mechanic exercise,
> Like dull narcotics, numbing pain.

These detached 'songs', genuine *cris de cœur*, short, poignant stabs of thought or feeling, are the nucleus round which the poem grew. They followed the rhythm in which the poet's emotion, at its acutest stage, found its most natural expression, and they dictated both the form and the metre of the work as a whole. The form roughly resembles that of a sonnet sequence. As the years went by and material accumulated, Tennyson conceived the idea—not altogether a happy one—of giving a certain unity to his 'wild and wandering cries' by representing them as an ordered progress from overwhelming sorrow to a cheerful resignation, from the chaos of doubt and despair to the security of a fixed faith. He condensed into three years the spiritual experience of fifteen, marked out a rough chronology by the repetition of three Christmases, three springs, and two anniversaries of his friend's death, composed variations, so to speak, on some of his original themes, amplified ideas, filled up gaps in the logical sequence of thought, prefixed a noble introduction, and added an epilogue which would have been better consigned to the waste paper basket. In doing all this he had tied himself from the first to a metre which, except when it is charged with emotion, borders on the trivial and is apt to become monotonous. Tennyson handled it with much skill, but, before they reach the end of the poem, most readers, I imagine, grow a little weary of its restricted rhythm and of the frequent repetition of the same rhyming words. In short, even in the hands of a master, the metre is not flexible enough to bear the long strain to which it is subjected.

In the completed work, called *In Memoriam*, we have Tennyson at his best and at his worst. There was a time when even his worst found admirers among his own contemporaries and their indiscriminate praise has helped to damage his reputation with a later generation. Genius always has its limitations, and Tennyson's were very marked. If we are to appreciate his solid achievement in English poetry, we must bear those limitations in mind, and take them into account. They are of several kinds.

(1) He was essentially a poet of the minor key. He found his truest inspiration in the mystery and pathos of life, not in its fullness, in looming mists and moaning seas, in 'old unhappy far-off things and battles long ago'. Whenever he attempted to preach in the major key, or to beat the drum, or to blow clarion blasts on the trumpet, he was apt to become ludicrous.

(2) In spite of such poems as *Ulysses* and *Rizpah*, and in spite of the numerous plays which he wrote in his last period, he had very little real dramatic sense. His contacts with the world of men and women were very restricted, and when he attempted to create an imaginary world of his own, he was inclined to people it with prigs. Hence he seldom found the revealing words which dramatic genius discovers for great occasions. Over the prostrate form of Guinevere his King Arthur can find nothing better to say than the devastating

> Lo, I forgive thee, as Eternal God
> Forgives.

o

Even in *In Memoriam* we find instances of this weakness; in xx, for example,

> The lesser griefs that may be said,
> > That breathe a thousand tender vows,
> > Are but as servants in a house
> Where lies the master newly dead;

> Who speak their feeling as it is,
> > And weep the fullness from the mind:
> > 'It will be hard,' they say, 'to find
> Another service such as this.'

But there are deeper griefs which suffer in silence, and

> . . . tears that at their fountain freeze;
> For by the hearth the children sit
> > Cold in that atmosphere of Death,
> > And scarce endure to draw the breath,
> Or like to noiseless phantoms flit:

> But open converse is there none,
> > So much the vital spirits sink
> > To see the vacant chair, and think,
> *'How good! how kind! and he is gone.'*

The italics are my own. That is not the language which expresses for bereavement its dreadful sense of finality, and the whole setting has the conventionality of melodrama.

(3) Tennyson had a very imperfect sense of humour and consequently plunged into bathos more often and more hopelessly than any other of the Olympians. Indeed, one often finds oneself wondering what those 'graceful jests' were like, which he was wont to exchange with Hallam. This

imperviousness to the ridiculous made him particularly liable to stumble whenever, as he loved to
do, he was indulging in domestic or parlour poetry.
The trivial events of family life, its simple hopes
and joys, its games, its picnics, its Christmas
gatherings, its births and marriages, *can* be treated
poetically, but they need skilful handling and a
very sure touch, more especially because the music
halls are constantly creating fun out of the same
material. Neither a lavish use of poetic synonyms
nor a stark simplicity will prevent pathos from
becoming bathos, if the sure touch is wanting.
Sandwiches are not made romantic merely by
being labelled a 'banquet in the distant woods',
nor does the naked use of 'Uncle' dissipate the
slightly comic associations which have gathered
round that word in certain connexions. We can
see Tennyson at his worst in LXXXIV where he is
considering what might have happened if his friend
had survived to marry his sister and become the
prosperous father of a family;

> I see thee sitting crown'd with good,
>   A central warmth diffusing bliss
>   In glance and smile, and clasp and kiss,
> On all the branches of thy blood;
>
> Thy blood, my friend, and partly mine;
>   For now the day was drawing on,
>   When thou should'st link thy life with one
> Of mine own house, and boys of thine
>
> Had babbled 'Uncle' on my knee.

Even before the days of central heating this would have passed as a parody of the domestic style. Nor does LXXXIX, which describes the vanished delight of Hallam's summer visits to Somersby, escape the pitfalls which such a theme strewed in the path of the poet.

> O bliss, when all in circle drawn
>   About him, heart and ear were fed
>   To hear him, as he lay and read
> The Tuscan poets on the lawn:

> Or in the all-golden afternoon
>   A guest, or happy sister, sung,
>   Or here she brought the harp and flung
> A ballad to the brightening moon.

I suppose that to the rising generation all, or almost all, of Tennyson's domestic poetry sounds slightly ridiculous; but to the sexagenarian some of it, at all events, carries associations and wakens memories which are gently soothing. It is true that our 'happy sisters' did not fling ballads to the brightening moon, but nearly all of us knew some dear old lady who still had a harp in her drawing-room—a harp no longer played on but kept in proper trim for the sake of 'use and wont', the sudden popping of whose strings denoted violent changes in the weather. Moreover in the Victorian era of large families far more self-sufficing and far less mobile than those of to-day, the lawn and the garden, the nearest copse and rivulet and meadow, played a larger part in the imagination and were more intimately woven into the fabric of life than is likely often to be possible in this age of rapid movement, nomadic habits, and suburbanized surroundings. Perhaps, if it survives at all, the parlour poetry of the Victorians will be studied chiefly for its antiquarian interest. But in inspired moments Tennyson did lift it on to a high level of art in which the trivial ceases to be trivial against a background of deep and poignant feeling. This is certainly the case in the first four stanzas of xxx:

> With trembling fingers did we weave
>   The holly round the Christmas hearth;
>   A rainy cloud possess'd the earth,
> And sadly fell our Christmas-eve.
>
> At our old pastimes in the hall
>   We gambol'd, making vain pretence
>   Of gladness, with an awful sense
> Of one mute Shadow watching all.
>
> We paused: the winds were in the beech:
>   We heard them sweep the winter land;
>   And in a circle hand-in-hand
> Sat silent, looking each at each.
>
> Then echo-like our voices rang;
>   We sung, tho' every eye was dim,
>   A merry song we sang with him
> Last year: impetuously we sang.

And although perhaps 'the fluttering urn' is not a particularly happy touch, and the description of the moths is over-elaborate and irrelevant, most of xcv has the same quality.

> By night we linger'd on the lawn,
>   For underfoot the herb was dry;
>   And genial warmth; and o'er the sky
> The silvery haze of summer drawn;
>
> And calm that let the tapers burn
>   Unwavering: not a cricket chirr'd:
>   The brook alone far-off was heard,
> And on the board the fluttering urn:
>
> And bats went round in fragrant skies,
>   And wheel'd or lit the filmy shapes
>   That haunt the dusk, with ermine capes
> And woolly breasts and beaded eyes;
>
> While now we sang old songs that peal'd
>   From knoll to knoll, where, couch'd at ease,
>   The white kine glimmer'd, and the trees
> Laid their dark arms about the field.
>
> But when those others, one by one,
>   Withdrew themselves from me and night,
>   And in the house light after light
> Went out, and I was all alone,
>
> A hunger seized my heart; I read
>   Of that glad year which once had been,
>   In those fall'n leaves which kept their green,
> The noble letters of the dead.

(4) Tennyson was always a conscious artist, but he was not always a consummate artist. At his best he was a master of great language and, even when uninspired, he could coin felicitous phrases. His worst poems are often strewn with magnificent lines. But he had a journalistic trick of trying to avoid the obvious or commonplace by a meretri-

cious use of words, and this trick, through lack of self-criticism, became with him a fixed and rather distressing habit. Such phrases as 'the sinless years that breathed beneath the Syrian blue', 'But where the path we walk'd began to slant the fifth autumnal slope', 'The blowing season' (i.e. March), 'Wandering isles of night' (i.e. sun-spots), 'The mimic picture's breathing grace' (i.e. *tableaux vivants*), 'The colours of the crimson prime', 'The life reorient out of dust' are journalism not poetry, and in many cases bad journalism. Moreover Tennyson does seem sometimes to have thought that by a deft use of language he could disguise in the unsavoury or the unsightly its unsavouriness or unsightliness, that by wreathing a pig-tub in roses he could endow it with a poetic value. His great contemporary, Robert Browning, was well aware that if pig-wash is to come into a poem at all, it must come in nakedly and unashamed as pig-wash; Tennyson would probably have called it 'the hoarded scraps that glut the swine'. In LXXXII, in order to evade the crudity of worms and corruption, he actually does say

> No lower life that earth's embrace
> May breed with him, can fright my faith;

and the effect is infinitely more repulsive than a plain statement of the fact that 'after the flesh worms destroy the body'. The worst of this trick of paraphrase, constantly repeated, is that it not only creates an atmosphere of artificiality, but

tends to make us suspicious of language which has
a real poetic value, and we find ourselves question-
ing such beautiful lines as

> Or where the kneeling hamlet drains
> The chalice of the grapes of God.

So much for his limitations; but, when he was
inspired, Tennyson could write with a grand
simplicity through which the tide of emotion runs
full and deep. Take vii for example:

> Dark house, by which once more I stand
> Here in the long unlovely street,
> Doors, where my heart was used to beat
> So quickly, waiting for a hand,
>
> A hand that can be clasp'd no more—
> Behold me, for I cannot sleep,
> And like a guilty thing I creep
> At earliest morning to the door.
>
> He is not here; but far away
> The noise of life begins again,
> And ghastly thro' the drizzling rain
> On the bald street breaks the blank day.

'He is not here'—*that* is the simple poignant
language of the heart in the misery of bereavement.

Or take again xi, written while the body of
Hallam was being brought by sea to England.

> Calm is the morn without a sound,
> Calm as to suit a calmer grief,
> And only thro' the faded leaf
> The chestnut pattering to the ground:

Calm and deep peace on this high wold,
    And on these dews that drench the furze,
    And all the silvery gossamers
That twinkle into green and gold:

Calm and still light on yon great plain
    That sweeps with all its autumn bowers,
    And crowded farms and lessening towers,
To mingle with the bounding main:

Calm and deep peace in this wide air,
    These leaves that redden to the fall;
    And in my heart, if calm at all,
If any calm, a calm despair:

Calm on the seas, and silver sleep,
    And waves that sway themselves in rest,
    And dead calm in that noble breast
Which heaves but with the heaving deep.

And yet again how much of quiet pathos and
poetry there is in xxviii.

The time draws near the birth of Christ:
    The moon is hid; the night is still;
    The Christmas bells from hill to hill
Answer each other in the mist.

Four voices of four hamlets round,
    From far and near, on mead and moor,
    Swell out and fail, as if a door
Were shut between me and the sound:

Each voice four changes on the wind,
    That now dilate, and now decrease,
    Peace and goodwill, goodwill and peace,
Peace and goodwill, to all mankind.

> This year I slept and woke with pain,
>   I almost wish'd no more to wake,
>   And that my hold on life would break
> Before I heard those bells again:
>
> But they my troubled spirit rule,
>   For they controll'd me when a boy;
>   They bring me sorrow touch'd with joy,
> The merry merry bells of Yule.

These are perfect numbers, and there are others which attain, or very nearly attain, to the same perfection, such, for instance, as X, XVIII, XIX, C, and CI. On the whole, I think, it is the earliest sections of the poem which leave the most lasting impression on the memory—the 'sweetest songs are those that tell of saddest thought'. Much of the rest is concerned with what the Elizabethans termed 'conceits', and which Tennyson himself calls short 'swallow-flights of song', in which he plays with the thoughts and fancies suggested by death and immortality. Many of these are pretty. One at least, unless my judgement is unduly influenced by early associations,[1] is something more than pretty, namely LXVII. At the risk of quoting too much, I shall quote it here in full.

> When on my bed the moonlight falls,
>   I know that in thy place of rest
>   By that broad water of the west,
> There comes a glory on the walls:

[1] I had to translate it into Latin verse in the *Twenty* at Rugby, and although it did not inspire me to write a respectable copy of Elegiacs, it first set me reading *In Memoriam*.

Thy marble bright in dark appears,
   As slowly steals a silver flame
   Along the letters of thy name,
And o'er the number of thy years.

The mystic glory swims away;
   From off my bed the moonlight dies;
   And closing eaves of wearied eyes
I sleep till dusk is dipt in gray:

And then I know the mist is drawn
   A lucid veil from coast to coast,
   And in the dark church like a ghost
Thy tablet glimmers to the dawn.

Of the philosophy of *In Memoriam* it is not necessary to speak. Tennyson was an imaginative singer, rather than a deep thinker; moreover he himself repeatedly deprecates the notion that he is attempting to be profound. He is only exploring ideas, as they occur to him, for a little way and not trying to establish a thesis. But one problem he states with extraordinary power and poetic insight, namely the difficulty of reconciling the God of Nature with a God of Love. This problem is still a skeleton in the cupboard of faith, but it was particularly alarming to the Victorians, because the advance of scientific knowledge had finally dissipated the comfortable belief that Nature was a sort of fairy godmother who 'kindly bounteous' cared for 'all her children', and the study of Biology had not yet delivered them from that other sympathetic fallacy, namely, that the hunted animal, that is to say, the animal which may at any moment become the prey of another, experiences exactly the same apprehensions and terrors as a civilized man would feel under similar conditions. This is how Tennyson faced the problem, squarely and without evasions.

LV

The wish, that of the living whole
    No life may fail beyond the grave,
    Derives it not from what we have
The likest God within the soul?

Are God and Nature then at strife,
    That Nature lends such evil dreams?
    So careful of the type she seems,
So careless of the single life;

That I, considering everywhere
    Her secret meaning in her deeds,
    And finding that of fifty seeds
She often brings but one to bear,

I falter where I firmly trod,
    And falling with my weight of cares
    Upon the great world's altar-stairs
That slope thro' darkness up to God,

I stretch lame hands of faith, and grope,
    And gather dust and chaff, and call
    To what I feel is Lord of all,
And faintly trust the larger hope.

LVI

'So careful of the type?' but no.
    From scarpèd cliff and quarried stone
    She cries, 'A thousand types are gone:
I care for nothing, all shall go.

'Thou makest thine appeal to me:
  I bring to life, I bring to death:
  The spirit does but mean the breath:
I know no more.' And he, shall he,

Man, her last work, who seem'd so fair,
  Such splendid purpose in his eyes,
  Who roll'd the psalm to wintry skies,
Who built him fanes of fruitless prayer,

Who trusted God was love indeed
  And love Creation's final law—
  Tho' Nature, red in tooth and claw
With ravine, shriek'd against his creed—

Who loved, who suffer'd countless ills,
  Who battled for the True, the Just,
  Be blown about the desert dust,
Or seal'd within the iron hills?

No more? A monster then, a dream,
  A discord. Dragons of the prime,
  That tare each other in their slime,
Were mellow music match'd with him.

O life as futile, then, as frail!
  O for thy voice to soothe and bless!
  What hope of answer, or redress?
Behind the veil, behind the veil.

Nor, I think, has the answering cry of the human
spirit, unproved and unprovable, ever been given
more movingly.

LIV

O yet we trust that somehow good
  Will be the final goal of ill,
  To pangs of nature, sins of will,
Defects of doubt, and taints of blood;

109

That nothing walks with aimless feet;
    That not one life shall be destroy'd,
    Or cast as rubbish to the void,
When God hath made the pile complete;

That not a worm is cloven in vain;
    That not a moth with vain desire
    Is shrivell'd in a fruitless fire,
Or but subserves another's gain.

Behold, we know not anything;
    I can but trust that good shall fall
    At last—far off—at last, to all,
And every winter change to spring.

So runs my dream: but what am I?
    An infant crying in the night:
    An infant crying for the light:
And with no language but a cry.

It is impossible to leave *In Memoriam* without a grateful mention of those frequent Nature-touches which give colour and atmosphere to the poem. It is not necessary for a poet to be a Natural Historian. Nobody enjoys Milton less because his nightingale 'tunes *her*' (not *his*) 'nocturnal note', and his flowers are apt to bloom out of their proper season. Tennyson, indeed, observed Nature more closely than most poets, and his accuracy must be counted to him for righteousness. But he was a poet of Nature, not because he observed minutely, but because he observed lovingly and with imagination. There is the cloud which

    Topples round the dreary West
    A looming bastion fringed with fire;

the day which issues howling out of night,

> With blasts that blow the poplar white
> And lash with storm the streaming pane;

there is the storm when

> The last red leaf is whirl'd away,
> The rooks are blown about the skies;

and this of the yew tree,

> To thee too comes the golden hour
> When flower is feeling after flower;
>
> .   .   .   .   .   .
>
> Thy gloom is kindled at the tips
> And passes into gloom again;

and autumn

> with the noise of rooks
> That gather in the waning woods;

or

> laying here and there
> A fiery finger on the leaves;

and spring, when

> rosy plumelets tuft the larch
> And rarely pipes the mounted thrush;

and the maple that 'burns itself away', and

> Deep tulips, dash'd with fiery dew,
> Laburnums, dropping-wells of fire;

and the winter day,

> A bitter day that early sank
> Behind a purple-frosty bank
> Of vapour;

and a great many more. None of them has quite
the magic of Shakespeare's

> daffodils
> That come before the swallow dares, and take
> The winds of March with beauty;

but they sing themselves into the memory and are
a constant source of pleasure to any one who loves
his own garden and the English landscape in all its
varying moods.

Such, then, is *In Memoriam*, a poem of great
moments rather than a great whole. Once it ranked
almost as a sacred book; to-day it suffers from the
undeserved neglect which is too often the sequel
of an exaggerated worship. But when the Victorians have been forgiven for being different from
their successors, and Tennyson for the pre-emi-
nence which he enjoyed in his own generation, *In
Memoriam* will have an assured and honourable
place in English literature, for it reflects in a vivid
way both the life and the thought of an arresting
epoch, it is rich in its response to natural beauty,
and, above all, it embodies a noble and a moving
expression of human love and human sorrow.

7. Shakespeare's Fairies

WITH the exception of Puck, the fairies of
A Midsummer Night's Dream are not the
fairies of whom stories were told by the winter fire
in Stratford-on-Avon when Shakespeare was a boy.
In all essentials they are the creation of his own
brain, children of that intuitive love of beauty
which, long before Wordsworth, had felt the
magic of the daffodil, and which, in the heart of
tragedy, made a lyric poem of Ophelia's death.
Not without reason did he call his fairyland a
vision and his play a dream.

> If we shadows have offended,
> Think but this, and all is mended,
> That you have but slumber'd here,
> While these visions did appear.

It is well to remember that fairies formed no
part of the country lore of ancient Greece and
Rome. They never danced in the plain of Attica,
nor held their revels among the Sabine hills. Their
home was far from the sunny shores of the Medi-
terranean, in the forest plains and mountains of
the barbarous North; and they were the offspring
less of the poetic fancy than of the superstitious
fears of the common people. As such, in sixteenth-
century England, as elsewhere, they bore the
stamp of their origin, 'instruments of darkness', a
menace to domestic peace, harbingers of misfortune,

Q

creatures of the night, and therefore to be dreaded. For in Elizabethan England popular imagination filled the night not with peace, but with terrors, terrors which nobody could describe more terrifyingly than Shakespeare himself. Graves gaped wide and let forth their sprites to glide through the church-way paths, witches held their sabbaths; the ghosts of malefactors haunted floods and crossroads, and murder stalked abroad.

> Now o'er the one half-world
> Nature seems dead, and wicked dreams abuse
> The curtain'd sleep; witchcraft celebrates
> Pale Hecate's offerings, and wither'd murder,
> Alarum'd by his sentinel the wolf,
> Whose howl's his watch, thus with his stealthy pace,
> With Tarquin's ravishing strides, towards his design
> Moves like a ghost.

Only at Christmas time, when 'our Saviour's birth is celebrated'

> no spirit dare stir abroad,
> The nights are wholesome, then no planets strike,
> No fairy takes nor witch hath power to charm,
> So hallow'd and so gracious is the time.

'No fairy takes' (i.e. casts spells); for among the sinister influences which night lets loose upon the world the fairies played their part: diminutive creatures, half human, half goblin; grotesque, if not repulsive, in appearance, and hostile, if not malicious, in disposition; less dangerous than witches, but capable of infinite mischief; stealing infants from the cradle and substituting some

114

cross-grained deformity, levying black-mail, and
casting spells which, if not fatal to life, added to its
trials and perplexities. A few among them had
acquired distinctive names and attributes, Queen
Mab, for example, a very different queen from
Queen Titania; and another who under various titles
played various parts in the affairs of men. As Hob-
goblin, or Robin Goodfellow, he was a spirit of
immense size and strength, Milton's 'lubber fiend'.
Well fed and properly humoured, he could be
serviceable to farmers, plough their fields by night
or thresh their corn. As Friar's Lantern, or Jack-
o'-my-lantern, he was a will-o'-the-wisp, luring
benighted travellers into floods and swamps. As
Puck he was the incarnation of mischief, playing
spiteful tricks, frightening the maids and causing
the work in farm and dairy to go all awry. Here
and there legend might tell of a good fairy, but
such goodness was the exception not the rule. The
'little people' were not friendly to mortals. They
might dance and revel like merry peasants, but
their mirth was ominous; a chance encounter
with them 'by some forest side or fountain' boded
no good.

Murder, ghosts, witches, goblins, and malicious
little sprites—well might the belated traveller spur
apace to gain the timely inn. 'But we', says Oberon
to Puck, 'are spirits of another sort.' For out of his
unpromising material Shakespeare created a new
world of strange beauty and peopled it with dainty
little spirits, wayward and wild but innocent of

malice, light as the air and beautiful as the flowers they tended, childlike, dreamlike. Our access to this fairyland lies through 'a wood near Athens', but its spiritual home is the forest of Arden, and Oberon and Titania still haunt the banks of the Warwickshire Avon.

To attempt to analyse a poet's dream is to rob it of its bloom. But it is interesting to note how Shakespeare handled his material. For the fairy scenes he reserved a poetry, lyrical in spirit and often in form, which contrasts sharply with the rhetoric of the lovers and the racy but unromantic prose of Bottom and his fellows. It gives to fairy-land its distinctive atmosphere. Sometimes it has all the magic with which Shakespeare could invest words. What could be more exquisite than

> The moon methinks looks with a watery eye,
> And, when she weeps, weeps every little flower
> Lamenting some enforced chastity.

Sometimes it has the homeliness, as well as the simplicity, of a nursery rhyme. Take, for example, Puck's

> Now the hungry lion roars,
>   And the wolf behowls the moon;
> Whilst the heavy ploughman snores,
>   All with weary work fordone;

or the last stanza of the fairy song:

> Weaving spiders come not here;
>   Hence, you long-legg'd spinners, hence!
> Beetles black, approach not near;
>   Worm nor snail, do no offence.

Chorus.

Philomel with melody
Sing in our sweet lullaby;
Lulla, lulla, lullaby, lulla, lulla, lullaby;
Never harm,
Nor spell nor charm,
Come our lovely lady nigh.

And always, unless perhaps when Puck is speaking, it is musical.

The fairies themselves and the even tinier elves, are a part of the beauty of the world which they people, the mysterious world of a summer night. They haunt fountains and hills and woods, but bear no resemblance to the Naiads, Oreads, and Dryads of Greek Mythology. They are not localized. The world is their parish, or rather their dancing ground. No sound betrays the tread of their tiny feet, and so swift are their motions that from India to Attica is for them but a step. Unlike the lesser divinities of classical myth, they are not a personification of natural forces; but they live very close to the heart of Nature, are, in fact, almost a part of her rhythmic pulse, and their dissensions bring havoc into the ordered march of the seasons. This is how Titania describes the dire consequences of her quarrel with Oberon:

These are the forgeries of jealousy:
And never, since the middle summer's spring,
Met we on hill, in dale, forest, or mead,
By paved fountain or by rushy brook,
Or in the beached margent of the sea,

To dance our ringlets to the whistling winds,
But with thy brawls thou hast disturb'd our sport.
Therefore the winds, piping to us in vain,
As in revenge, have suck'd up from the sea
Contagious fogs; which, falling in the land,
Have every pelting river made so proud,
That they have overborne their continents.

The result has been ruined harvests, drowned fields, and empty folds; while the moon, 'the governess of floods', angry at this encroachment on her prerogatives, has 'washed all the air' so that 'rheumatic diseases do abound' among unhappy mortals.

And thorough this distemperature we see
The seasons alter: hoary-headed frosts
Fall in the fresh lap of the crimson rose;
And on old Hiems' thin and icy crown
An odorous chaplet of sweet summer buds
Is, as in mockery, set; the spring, the summer,
The childing autumn, angry winter, change
Their wonted liveries; and the mazed world,
By their increase, now knows not which is which:
And this same progeny of evils comes
From our debate, from our dissension;
We are their parents and original.

Of Shakespeare's fairies Puck was no doubt the favourite among Elizabethan audiences; but he is the least poetical. He was too deeply rooted in popular tradition to be treated otherwise than traditionally. But, though he retains his aliases and his power to assume fantastic shapes, he ceases

to be a malicious goblin and becomes merely a
light-hearted, if somewhat mischievous imp, the
'merry wanderer of the night', bent on a rather
boisterous type of fun, the 'lob of spirits', Oberon's
jester, the comic man among the fairies. As an
immortal spirit he has a profound contempt for
mortals, especially for a churl or lack-o'-love; but
for lovers, especially when, like Helena, they are
young and pretty, he has a warm corner in his
heart, and he is as happily employed in bringing
their troubles to an end, as in scaring the 'hempen
home-spuns' back to Stratford, or rather to Athens.
In short, a high-spirited little rascal, rather a
nuisance at times to men and maids and to elderly
aunts telling sad stories by the fire-side, but not
vindictive, and, on the whole, more amusing than
formidable.

With Oberon and Titania Shakespeare had a
free hand; they were his own children, and he
could deal with them as he pleased. He makes
them half English fairy, and half Greek god. As
fairies they lead the nightly revels of their followers
or, unseen and unheard, bless the bride-beds of
favoured mortals; as gods they can assume human
form and associate with kings and heroes—or is
this only make-believe, part of a game in which,
like children, they play at being grown-ups? In
any case, their attitude to men is entirely friendly.
Titania feels remorse for the misfortunes in which
their quarrels have involved poor humanity;
Oberon is at once interested in the fate of the

lovers and insists that their story shall have a happy ending. Their manners are those of the most polished aristocrats. Even when they are quarrelling they observe a decorous reticence, and, unlike the human lovers, never indulge in harsh and violent abuse. It is characteristic too of Oberon that he speaks of Bottom, asleep in Titania's bower, as 'this Athenian swain', and orders that he shall be relieved of his ass's head and sent back happily to Athens.

They are both exquisite beings. Titania has something of the delicate beauty of a wild flower; she is 'our lovely lady', 'our lovely queen'. But what constitutes their peculiar charm is that with all their supernatural powers and their high breeding they have the minds and psychology of children. It is true that they can speak the language of sex, sometimes with Elizabethan frankness; Titania, for example:

> His mother was a votaress of my order:
> And, in the spiced Indian air, by night,
> Full often hath she gossip'd by my side;
> And sat with me on Neptune's yellow sands,
> Marking the embarked traders on the flood;
> When we have laugh'd to see the sails conceive
> And grow big-bellied with the wanton wind.

And they romance about their love affairs with famous men and women. But their love is the love of children, passionate, capricious, sexless. The fairies have no offspring.

Like children, too, they quarrel over the possession of a toy, in this case a beautiful little Indian page, called 'a changeling boy', but not really so; for he is the child of the above-mentioned votaress, and Titania is rearing him out of affection for his mother, who died in giving him birth.

And they both speak the loveliest of language. Here is Oberon:

> I know a bank whereon the wild thyme blows,
> Where oxlips and the nodding violet grows;
> Quite over-canopied with luscious woodbine,
> With sweet musk-roses, and with eglantine;
> And there the snake throws her enamell'd skin,
> Weed wide enough to wrap a fairy in.
> There sleeps Titania sometime of the night,
> Lull'd in these flowers with dances and delight.

And here Titania:

> Come, now a roundel and a fairy song,
> Then, for the third part of a minute, hence;
> Some to kill cankers on the musk-rose buds;
> Some war with rere-mice for their leathern wings,
> To make my small elves coats, and some keep back
> The clamorous owl, that nightly hoots, and wonders
> At our quaint spirits. Sing me now asleep;
> Then to your offices, and let me rest.

And again:

> Be kind and courteous to this gentleman;
> Hop in his walks, and gambol in his eyes;
> Feed him with apricocks and dewberries,
> With purple grapes, green figs, and mulberries;
> The honey-bags steal from the humble-bees,
> And for night-tapers crop their waxen thighs,

R

And light them at the fiery glow-worm's eyes,
To have my love to bed and to arise;
And pluck the wings from painted butterflies,
To fan the moonbeams from his sleeping eyes:
Nod to him, elves, and do him courtesies.

And so, with their attendant trains of fairies and elves, they flit from hemisphere to hemisphere, filling the emptiness of night with mirth and music, 'chasing darkness like a dream', though Oberon, in the guise of a forester, will often linger on some sea-shore, to watch the sun rising from his ocean bed.

To introduce Bottom into this world of fragile beauty, Bottom, with his crude realism, his gross appetite, his sententious humour, and his devastating yawns: to draw out all the fun latent in this absurd contrast, without breaking the spell of fairyland or impairing its charm—this was a master stroke, possible only for one who was both a consummate poet and a consummate humorist. We laugh till our sides ache, but we never cease to be conscious (at least when we are reading) of the mysterious loveliness of the fairies and their bower, while the ass's head helps to remind us that we are in an enchanted world. Nor does Titania, in love with the 'bully' weaver, lose for one moment her natural dignity and charm, any more than does a little girl who is enamoured of a golly-wog, or who falls asleep clasping her Teddy bear in her arms. She remains 'our lovely lady', 'our lovely queen'.

Like Dogberry in *Much Ado*, Bottom gains much

by being acted. But the fairies . . . ? So far as I am aware there is no authentic tradition as to how Shakespeare staged his fairies. Presumably he made use of children, that is to say of boys, for the convention which forbade the stage to women would hardly have tolerated little girls. An adult Oberon or Titania is fatal to all illusion. So for that matter is an adult Puck. But even with children to fill the parts—and none but children can fill them adequately—we do not get the real fairy-land. It matters little that Oberon cannot suddenly become invisible, or Puck materialize out of nothing and vanish into nowhere; but the problem of size is vital, if the thing said is to correspond with the thing seen, and the difficulties are insuper-able. To a fairy the cowslips are tall, and to an elf still taller. The tiniest child cannot wrap itself in the sloughed skin of a grass-snake, or hide in an acorn-cup. Oberon and Titania, it is true, can assume what shape and size they please, but 'in their own dimensions, like themselves', they are something very small, only a little larger than their attendant fairies, and in the 'wood near Athens' they are in their own dimensions. Titania, asleep in her bower, has to be guarded, not from bears and wolves, but from spiders, black-beetles, and snails.

Shakespeare was before all things a poet, and he would never sacrifice the poetry of his drama-tic conceptions to the limitations of the theatre. But the truth is that when he tried to bring his fairyland on to the stage, he was attempting the impossible. No doubt he knew this, and the knowledge did not deter him—for which we may be thankful. He had dreamt of a world of minute beauty, one, too, in which time and distance are annihilated, shapes interchangeable, and where magic becomes the law of Nature. But such worlds are visible only to that 'inward eye, which is the bliss of solitude'. The fairy scenes are wonderful literature, but they wilt behind the footlights, and 'fade into the light of common day'.

And so the play, when acted, tends to become the play of Bottom, the King of all Shakespearian clowns, for to most people, I imagine, the long-drawn-out wrangles of the lovers grow rather tedious, while Theseus and Hippolyta, though figures of a high romance, take little part in the action. It is not the insubstantial pageant of fairyland, but the very substantial one of Pyramus and Thisbe which triumphs on the stage.

But the fairies have the last word in the play, and, on the whole, they have had it in fairy literature—at any rate in England. In *A Midsummer Night's Dream* Shakespeare purged them of their grossness, touched them with beauty, Hellenized them, and made them an attractive theme for poets and for children. Years afterwards in *The Tempest*, which was probably written at Stratford, he recaptured the mood which had inspired his earlier play and gave us Ariel, a daintier spirit than Puck, but not quite so remote a cousin as some admirers would have us believe. Puck would have been quite in his element scaring the shipwrecked conspirators and dealing faithfully with Caliban; and Ariel, released from Prospero's isle, would not have been out of place in the enchanted forest near Athens, and that fairy world Shakespeare called into being with his magic wand, when he was twenty-nine years old, and still only on the threshold of his amazing career.

8. Gain and Loss

IT is probable that few people in any generation ever reach the age of seventy without feeling with Wordsworth 'that there has passed away a glory from the earth'. For, even when the stage is set for progress, evolution brings losses as well as gains, and the septuagenarian is likely to be more conscious of the loss than of the gain. This must be particularly true of any one who grew up among the Victorians and has survived to spend his latter days among the neo-Georgians; for in those years the newer 'glories' that replace the old ones have followed each other with such rapidity, that he finds it hard to adapt his vision to all of them or even to recognize them as 'glories' at all. It is the penalty of age to fall behind the times, but if we admit that our slowness to appreciate much of what is new in the world of to-day is probably due to our mental stiffness rather than to superior taste or a maturer wisdom, we shall perhaps be pardoned for dwelling more fondly on the past than on the present.

For the Victorian past really did contain many good things which can now be enjoyed no more. For my own part I cannot honestly believe that anybody has tasted the fullness of life who has not driven down Oxford Street in the 1880's in a holiday mood on a summer afternoon in a really well-appointed hansom cab, with a horse which might once have been a Derby winner, and a driver who knew how to drive. The jingle of the harness, and the beat of hooves on the hard asphalt, sounded musically in the ear; the pace was fast— faster than anything else upon the street, which is what really matters, but not so fast that one could not see and be seen, and there was a sense of opulence, very grateful to whoever earned his living by the sweat of brow or brain, which is wholly absent from the modern taxi-cab.

Those were the days when the shadows of evening were beginning to gather round the Victorian era, when Tennyson was no longer 'the bard' for youth, and such whiskers as survived were nearly always grey. But they were still the days of large families and a large hospitality; of cheap coal, cheap clothes, and cheap service, and, in the country, of home-made jams, bread, butter, and of home-cured hams and bacon; when servants came for low wages and stayed for a lifetime, to become part of the family, proud of its traditions, and jealous of its honour; when flowers held up their heads, roses smelled divinely, and a bunch of sweet peas would scent a room; when apples grew and ripened on unblighted trees without being sprayed, and bees made honey instead of dying of Isle of Wight disease; when the costs of a public school education were still comparatively light, and science, which has done so much to make them heavy, was still called 'Stinks' and held in small repute; in short, the Golden Age of the professional classes.

But it was not the Golden Age of the poor, and that is a sobering thought for a Victorian. Part at least of the cheapness was wrung from bare-footed, ragged, unhealthy children in mean slum streets; for dire distress and poverty among many of the industrial workers were the first fruits of the Industrial System, as they may possibly be the last. The worst blunder of the Victorians was not their sentimental idealization of women, but their unsentimental faith in the Industrial Revolution. They believed that a continuous increase of material wealth and a soaring birth-rate necessarily meant national prosperity; they believed in cheap labour, they believed in Political Economy, they believed in Free Trade which, however sound it may have been commercially, was an inhuman creed, because it thought in terms of economic law and not of flesh and blood. They did *not* believe in beauty for its own sake as a vital element in a healthy spiritual life. They would have manufactured boots on the tops of all the Lake mountains, if boots could have been manufactured there more cheaply than at Northampton. They began the devastation of the country-side, which has been going on ever since. It was not their indifferent taste in furniture which made them dangerous, but their surrenders to ·Mammon.

But although Carlyle was still thundering anathemas, and Ruskin lifted up his voice and wept, we who reached our teens in the 1870's did not realize whither we were being led, and we found life very good, and very exciting. Nothing hurts us so much as to be told by the rising generation that we lived tamely in a tame age of debased tastes and paralysing conventions.

The pioneer of yesterday is always the fossil of to-day; but in our youth we felt ourselves to be pioneers always gaining new ground. We rebelled against the worst traditions of the Sabbath, and we helped women on to their first bicycles. In music we began by adoring Handel and passed on to Bach, Beethoven and, later, Brahms; in art we started with the Soul's Awakening, and then discovered Whistler and Rossetti, not to mention the great forgotten masters of the Dutch and Italian schools; in poetry we began by abusing all modern poets who were not Tennyson, and afterwards transferred our allegiance to Swinburne and Browning. Many of us stopped discovering with Brahms and Rossetti, and some of us with Browning; our wings could carry us no farther. To-day, when I hear the same audience applauding Bach and Bax, with a touch of added warmth for Bax, I conclude that they were born with an appreciation of Bach, and are discovering Bax. I cannot follow with the young. My eye is too dim to discern new forms of painting, my ear too rigid to catch new rhythms in music.

But I seem to note in most forms of modern art a certain austerity, a horror of sentiment, a dread of being pretty; and I cannot help remembering that Puritanism is capable of leading, not to beauty, but to bleakness. It once led our forefathers from the Gothic Cathedrals to the Baptist Chapel. But I do not pretend to judge what I cannot understand.

What I am sure of is, that I and my fellow Victorians had many enjoyments which are denied to the present generation. For one thing travel abroad, being less easy and less comfortable, was more of an adventure. The flesh is weak, and will always choose the quickest, surest, and least fatiguing way of reaching its destination, but delays, uncertainties, and discomforts, which have to be endured and overcome, give a greater thrill to achievement and a sharper edge to memory. There were, too, nearer home far more places which were difficult of access. We had the satisfaction of discovering England. Much of Cornwall was still virgin soil for the holiday-maker in the 1870's and 80's. There is a pleasure—a selfish one, perhaps, but still a pleasure—in discovering a new place which none of one's friends or acquaintances has yet discovered, planting one's own flag on it, occupying, exploring, making it one's own. And for the traveller on foot or on a bicycle, there was a far greater variety of local colour, of dress, of food, of speech. To-day, whether she issues from a castle or a cottage, every woman is dressed exactly like every other woman; the missing half of a cake or a bun could be supplied from any tea-table between John-o'-Groats and Land's End; and everybody says 'Right-o'. The standardization of modern life has not made for picturesqueness.

I observe that the young people of to-day find a pleasure in doing gregariously some of the things which we used to do alone, or with a single companion. I met recently in the Forest of Dean a party of some twenty 'hikers'. They were not perfectly equipped for enjoyment, for the girls had exposed the maximum of bare flesh in a locality where swarms of voracious flies are the rule and not the exception, but they were obviously enjoying themselves in a simple, healthy way. The gregarious instinct is every bit as respectable as the reaction from it, and it is as old as Chaucer's Canterbury Pilgrims. But there are things which cannot be enjoyed gregariously, the study of wild life, the balm of silence, 'the quietness of thought'. These are less easy to come by than of old; yet in an age so rich in mechanical noises as the present it is good from time to time to be somewhere, where one can say,

'The winds come to me from the fields of sleep'.

It is, of course, an excellent thing that city dwellers, poor as well as rich, should be able to pour out in their thousands to the country-side and to the seaside. But there is an attraction about a lonely shore which disappears with its loneliness, and there are things and places which cannot be enjoyed by crowds, because their beauty is too fragile, or on too small a scale, to survive numbers. Wild flowers vanish under the trampling of many feet and the clutch of many hands; Cheddar

S 2

Gorges, blocked with charabancs and alive with
trippers, cease to be Cheddar Gorges, and become
a poor substitute for a crowded thoroughfare in
some great city; even the remoter cliffs suffer from
the invasion of the many. The crowds depart, but
they leave their litter behind them, as they leave it
everywhere. There are places on the sea-shore
where a man may walk knee-deep in rubbish. The
Victorians suffered from an excess of modesty and
ridiculous bathing-machines, but they did not have
to bathe in sewage-tainted seas, and dress themselves amidst refuse.

I shall be told that for all these losses there are
compensating gains; that adventure, for instance,
though it is no longer sought on foot, or on the
push-bike, or in the train, is found on the motor-
cycle, in the car, and in the aeroplane, more costly,
but still more exciting. With a yearly casualty list
for the road alone of 6,000 killed and 180,000
injured, I do not question either the adventure or
the excitement; I am only maintaining that things
which were enjoyable can no longer be enjoyed, or
are at least more difficult of attainment.

And in this connexion I venture to add that I
think we got more fun out of our games, because
we took them less seriously. If we hit at a ball
which should have been played, or tackled some
one round the neck instead of round the ankles,
there was nobody to tell us that we had been false
to our King, our Country, our School, and our
House. Specialization, intensive training, and a

mistaken estimate of their moral value, are making games irksome to boys. This exaggeration of a late Victorian cult makes for efficiency, but mars enjoyment; and games were meant to be enjoyed. Some 50 per cent. of public schoolboys have learnt instead to loathe cricket; before long a similar number will probably loathe football, which is a pity.

Is England a happier country than it was seventy years ago? Many positive gains stare one cheerfully in the face. The children of the poor are certainly happier. They are better fed, better clothed, better cared for, better loved. And of their fathers, whenever the industrial machine is functioning normally, fewer have any real injustice to brood over. The Social Services, too, have been vastly extended, and, though they tend to make the beneficiaries forget that they have duties to, as well as claims upon, the State, the gains vastly outweigh the losses. But happiness is an imponderable state of mind, and it depends far less on the realization of material values than the indigent are apt to suppose.

The satisfaction of an innate, though often unconscious, desire for beauty is an essential part of real happiness, and just as those who live in unventilated rooms become cross and headachey without realizing that they are breathing a vitiated atmosphere, so people who are condemned to live in ugly, sordid surroundings grow up discontented and rebellious without knowing the reason why.

During the last seventy years for a large section of our countrymen there has been an appreciable loss of beauty. Most of our great industrial towns are past praying for, but the progressive mutilation of the countryside is one of the most alarming signs of the times. I do not wish to exaggerate; the beauty of England, in its quiet way the most beautiful of all countries, will not be destroyed in a day. But in almost every shire the work of destruction goes on apace. Oaks and beeches are being felled, copses are vanishing, historic mansions are being demolished and their parks converted into bungalow towns; picturesque villages are ceasing to be picturesque; roads are being stripped of their trees and straightened out for the passage of thundering lorries and buses, and wherever the bus goes, houses spring up instead of hedges. Whatever has a market value is passing into the hands of the speculative builder. There are few people, whether in provincial towns or villages, or farms, who do not miss some of the old amenities of life. Everywhere there is noise, confusion, and a lavish display of bad taste. It is no consolation to be told that there are people who can build cottages and plan estates that are not eye-sores. With rare exceptions they are not the people who are building the cottages and planning the estates. There are whole tracts along the south coast which resemble nothing on earth so much as a great gooseberry bush ravaged by white caterpillars.

This short-sighted destruction of beauty, this

failure to recognize that beauty is worth preserving for its own sake, and cannot be preserved without some sacrifice of material gain, is closely allied to the habit of measuring standards of living by the number of material possessions which they include. Science, which claims to supply wants, is in reality always creating new needs, and the luxury of to-day becomes the necessity of to-morrow. Indeed, the whole purpose of scientific industrialism is to create needs, in order to be able to supply them at a profit by mass production. Diogenes carried his principles to extreme lengths, and it would be preferable to live in a palace rather than in a tub; but there is much practical wisdom, as well as spiritual truth, in the recognition that, after a certain point, the multiplication of material possessions does not make for happiness. The difficulty is to fix the point; but it remains true that, although man cannot live without bread, he cannot live by bread alone. The Victorians were certainly not less happy because they were obliged to live more simply.

There is one very large assumption which underlies all modern ideas of progress and which is much less convincing to the Victorian than to his offspring, namely, that every new mechanical invention which saves human effort, intelligence, and manual dexterity, marks a step forward in civilization and is a benefit to humanity. The old Victorian is haunted by the fear that the fool-proof machine may end in making fools of men. Hitherto man has found his chief incentive to effort, and the most effective stimulus to his imagination and intelligence, in his daily work. In proportion as his effort, skill, and intelligence are transferred to a machine functioning automatically, he tends to cease to be a worker and becomes a watcher. Eventually he will have to earn his daily bread by a few hours of soul-destroying drudgery and to live by his leisure. There are enthusiasts who regard this prospect without misgivings, in spite of the fact that hitherto few people have been able to make a profitable use of an unrestricted leisure. The effect of such leisure on the unemployed of to-day is hardly encouraging. One may well wonder how the average man is going to find the large culture, the wide interests, the intellectual enterprise, which will be necessary when his leisure ceases to be a change of occupation, and becomes the only field for the exercise of his intelligent activities. One may even wonder how he is going to find the brains. One can only note that, up to the present, little is being done to fit him for the change, the most momentous in human history; for secondary education, instead of growing broader, grows narrower, more specialized, more technical.

Mechanical inventiveness is the triumph of our age. Almost daily it is changing the outward appearance of life. The more timid of us would like to feel surer that we are being whirled along to Eldorado and not to a precipice. Perhaps even others than septuagenarians would not be sorry if the inventors were to take a holiday, for to most people there comes a saturation point, at which they would like to assimilate and enjoy what they have already got. My own saturation point came long ago. If the clock could be stopped, I should have stopped it in the days when the discovery of pneumatic tyres had made the push-bicycle the king of the roads. It was a less attractive animal than the horse, but it cost much less and had a wider range. We needed no licence for it, it made no noise, it did not smell, we did not feel that we were bound to use it, but when we did, it provided us with exercise as well as with amusement. With the wind behind us, and on a road which was then considered good, we felt that we were devouring space; but as we were not, our crashes, when we crashed, were seldom fatal. There was nothing on the King's highway that we could not overtake and pass with ease. We gloried in our strength and swiftness. It was a black day, when from a thick cloud of dust, with the grinding of machinery and the stench of oil, the first motor-car drove us into the hedge; for more than anything else, it marked for us the dawn of a new era which was not ours.